Quarterly Essay

Quarterly Essay is published four times a year by Black Inc., an imprint of Schwartz Books Pty Ltd. Publisher: Morry Schwartz.

ISBN 9781760643560 ISSN 1444-884x

Subscriptions – 1 year print & digital (4 issues): $79.95 within Australia incl. GST. Outside Australia $119.95. 2 years print & digital (8 issues): $149.95 within Australia incl. GST. 1 year digital only: $49.95.

Payment may be made by Mastercard or Visa, or by cheque made out to Schwartz Books. Payment includes postage and handling.

To subscribe, fill out and post the subscription card or form inside this issue, or subscribe online:

quarterlyessay.com
subscribe@blackincbooks.com
Phone: 61 3 9486 0288

Correspondence should be addressed to:

The Editor, Quarterly Essay
22–24 Northumberland Street
Collingwood VIC 3066 Australia
Phone: 61 3 9486 0288 / Fax: 61 3 9011 6106
Email: quarterlyessay@blackincbooks.com

Editor: Chris Feik. Management: Elisabeth Young. Publicity: Anna Lensky. Design: Guy Mirabella. Assistant Editor: Kirstie Innes-Will. Production Coordinator: Marilyn de Castro. Typesetting: Typography Studio.

Printed in Australia by McPherson's Printing Group. The paper used to produce this book comes from wood grown in sustainable forests.

"Rapacity reigns, passions are obeyed, the world is given priority, and each person admires his own opinion."

—Prophet Muhammad

"You start to think of contempt as a virus."

—Zadie Smith

"We gasp for air among people who believe they are absolutely right, whether it be in their machines or their ideas. And for all who cannot live without dialogue and the friendship of other human beings, this silence is the end of the world."

—Albert Camus

UNCIVIL WARS

How Contempt Is Corroding Democracy

Waleed Aly & Scott Stephens

Something's amiss, isn't it? "We may live in the first period of human history where every demographic feels that they are somehow being violated and victimized," writes Mark Manson, capturing something at once familiar and bewildering about our moment. This is not simply one of those revolutionary moments when the long-downtrodden rise up against their oppressors – as witnessed, for example, at the height of the civil-rights struggle in the 1960s, or a century earlier with the women's suffrage movement. Sure, that may be part of the story, but such a summary would prove too partial.

This is instead a moment when almost any issue can draw sharp lines between us: climate change, taxation, the language on a medical form. It is now entirely common for each of the opposing sides of a vociferous debate to consider themselves shamed and silenced, unable to speak without being branded in some malevolent way. In this respect (and perhaps only in this respect), advocates speaking of the existential erasure of transgender people speak the same language as gender-critical feminists who complain of the erasure of women under the axioms of gender fluidity. Black American activists talk of the existential threat they face at the hands of a white-supremacist culture, while repeated surveys reveal a majority of white Americans think anti-white discrimination is as bad as or worse than discrimination against blacks and other minorities. Among the white working class, the figure rises to about two-thirds.

So often we distil this as Sally, a viewer of the BBC's *Question Time*, did in a tweet to the show in 2019: "Why is everyone, so angry about everything, all of the time?" Predictably, that tweet invited its own anger, with respondents sneering at Sally's excessive use of commas. But punctuation aside, everyone seems desperate to answer the question. The English-language internet is awash with articles diagnosing the incandescent tone of public debate and doling out advice on how best to handle it, especially with family and friends. That last point is fundamental, not least in the United States, where partisan division has hardened so much that it is now frequently terminating friendships and leaving family members unable to converse. In 2016, the Pew Research Center showed just how rapidly and deeply Democratic and Republican voters' mutual suspicion and disdain was advancing: majorities of each now had a "very unfavourable" view of the other – more than double what it was at the turn of the millennium. By 2020, Pew found that Biden and Trump voters hardly knew each other. A mere 3 per cent of each had "a lot" of friends who supported the opposing candidate. Around 40 per cent of each said they had no friends at all who did. Add to them those who have only "a few" such friends, and the number on either side approaches 80 per cent.

Australian polarisation is not quite so severe, and has less voluminous data to measure it, but we can easily discern a similar direction of travel. "It's absolutely staggering," declared Andrew Charlton, a former senior adviser to Prime Minister Kevin Rudd and now Labor MP, in 2018. "The warning lights on the dashboard of our democracy are blinking red. It's very hard to constructively govern in an electorate that is so divided." Surveys show that voters regard the major parties as becoming more politically extreme, even though analysis of party policies, speeches and voting records by Political Compass demonstrates that ideologically they have scarcely moved. This underscores data from the 2013 Australian Election Study: in asking voters to rank their own political leanings from 0 (very left-wing) to 10 (very right-wing), it revealed increasing numbers who place themselves far from the statistical mean. Since the study began in 1996, Labor and Greens voters have placed themselves further to the left, Liberals have been largely consistent, and Nationals voters place themselves further to the right.

Data aside, we already intuit this. Public broadcaster SBS can happily publish a comment piece on "How to survive your conservative relatives this Christmas," presumably because this seems a familiar concern. The aftermath of the 2019 federal election, in which Queensland played a decisive role, saw a proliferation of tweets and memes calling for a "Quexit," demanding Australia "cut them loose!" This, we think, was a joke, along the lines of "What the hell is wrong with Queensland?" But it was taken seriously enough to prompt earnest think-pieces pleading with Australians, "don't judge, try to understand us."

So, anger, sure. Rage, or even outrage, yes. All these are such common descriptions of our age because they capture something of the truth. And yet they miss something, too. People have always gotten angry at their loved ones, but they remained loved. Something deeper is going on here, when it leads not merely to flashes of disagreement, but to a more permanent alienation. Whatever's amiss in public conversation, we don't seem quite to have diagnosed it precisely.

On 9 September 2016, amid the maelstrom of America's presidential election campaign, Hillary Clinton gave a campaign speech at a fundraiser in which she made what quickly became an infamous observation about Donald Trump's supporters. "You know, to just be grossly generalistic, you could put half of Trump's supporters into what I call a basket of deplorables," she said, to laughter from the audience. "Right? They're racist, sexist, homophobic, xenophobic, Islamophobic – you name it. And unfortunately, there are people like that ... Now some of those folks – they are irredeemable, but thankfully, they are not America." By contrast, the other half – the "other basket" – had

Clinton's sympathy. They were people who felt "let down" by government and the economy, "people we have to understand and empathize with."

The furore was immediate. "I regret saying 'half' – that was wrong," Clinton said in a statement, which of course didn't specify what proportion would have been better. Simultaneously, though, her campaign cited polling showing Trump supporters had negative attitudes towards Latinos, African Americans and Muslims.

"How can you unite the country if you've written off tens of millions of Americans?" asked CNN's Anderson Cooper during the next month's presidential debate. Clinton replied that her argument was not with Trump's supporters but with Trump himself. But his supporters didn't see it that way. They defiantly adopted the label, wearing T-shirts emblazoned with "Deplorable" and hats saying "Proud to Be Deplorable." At a rally, Trump walked onto the stage to the sound of "Do You Hear the People Sing?," the revolutionary anthem from *Les Misérables*. On the screen behind him was a photoshopped image from the musical with the original flags replaced by a mixture of Trump and American flags, beneath the parodic heading *Les Deplorables*.

It was a turning point. Clinton later conceded it contributed to her defeat, but people who worked on her campaign were more forthright. "All hell broke loose," wrote a Clinton pollster in the *Boston Globe*, identifying it as the moment:

> I saw more undecided voters shift to Trump than any other, when it all changed, when voters began to speak differently about their choice. It wasn't FBI Director James Comey, Part One or Part Two; it wasn't Benghazi or the e-mails or Bill Clinton's visit with Attorney General Loretta Lynch on the tarmac.

This potent response, much like our public conversation, is rooted in something more than mere anger. Voters get angry at politicians all the time, and in any event, Trump's supporters seemed to be having great fun with the label rather than becoming angry. It drew on something else – something that all the other potentially scandalous allegations hurled at Clinton in the campaign didn't. And it was Trump's senior communications adviser, Jason Miller, who identified it with precision: "Just when Hillary Clinton said she was going to start running a positive campaign, she ripped off her mask and revealed her true contempt for everyday Americans."

There it was. Contempt.

"Deplorable" and "irredeemable" are words with enormous weight. They go to the very worth of people. They signal a kind of excision, a total severance between the describer and the described, even a desire for excommunication. "It would have been different if she had said, 'Half the Trump voters are *behaving* deplorably'," said Jonathan Allen – co-author of a study of the 2016 campaign – to *The Washington Post*. Anderson Cooper had put his question insightfully: it was one thing to criticise millions of Americans, but quite something else to write them off as people. No doubt having honed the line of attack carefully, Trump was incisive in his response. Here he is, standing in front of his *Les Deplorables* banner, on Clinton's use of "irredeemable": "Boy, that second word is tough. You don't hear that as much, but that means you're never going to come back, folks ... Irredeemable, they don't talk about that one, but that was, to me, pretty bad."

You're never going to come back, much like that friend or family member who is cut off, or the entire state people want to excise. A 2020 survey found that 81 per cent of Republicans think the Democratic Party has been taken over by socialists. Some 78 per cent of Democrats think the Republican Party has been taken over by racists. Nearly half of independent voters agree with each of these assessments. You're never going to come back from that, either. At this point, each takes the other to belong to a group that cannot be engaged, that cannot be redeemed, that simply must be vanquished. The problem isn't merely polarisation. It's the contempt with which each side regards the other. Once that happens, political debate ceases to be an exchange, heated or otherwise. It ceases to be about persuasion. It becomes existential. This, we suspect, is what people are trying to capture when they say things like "everyone is angry about everything all the time." It might be truer to say everyone feels existentially slighted all the time; that we're caught in a cycle of deep mutual condemnation, uninterested in hearing each other's explanations, defences, counterclaims, hurling not just accusations, but convictions. In short, writing each other off. Contempt – more than just anger – is what's amiss.

Australian politics has had no shortage of contemptuous episodes, led by politicians and echoed by their followers. Here it would be easy – and accurate – to cite the sexist hectoring of Julia Gillard during her premiership, or the frequent dehumanising of asylum seekers in which politicians were prepared to accuse some of them of setting themselves on fire or throwing their children into the sea as a cynical strategy to cheat their way to Australia. But it has also infected our climate wars, in which ardent demands to shut down coalmines, for instance, tend to come from those who stand to lose the least from this, with little regard for the communities whose history and identities are so bound up in the coal industry – viewing them as a problem to be overcome rather than people whose lives and concerns are to be taken seriously. This took an issue on which some agreement may have been brokered and made it an identity conflict, and ultimately a culture war. So, in the words of the Labor-aligned mayor of Isaac Regional Council in central Queensland, "to date, it's been an 'us and them' discussion, not a 'we' discussion . . . We're not talking about not setting a target. We're not naive to climate change. Our message is, 'We feel invisible'." That is why the "Stop Adani" convoy from Tasmania to North Queensland during the 2019 election campaign would have seemed contemptuous to so many. Here was a group of southern interlopers, with no deep concern for the lives of those up north, demanding they forgo what many will have seen as an economic opportunity, while their own jobs in the knowledge economy were secure. Local politicians credit this convoy with solidifying the swing away from Labor in Queensland that year. This sort of approach also underwrites the rhetoric of Nationals leaders – itself contemptuous – that banging on about climate change is the preserve of "inner-city raving lunatics." None of this has been productive.

And yet, contempt continues to grow in our public conversation as a standard way of doing business. More than that, as a moral way of doing business. When people condemn others, including by ending relationships with family and friends, they are unlikely to feel they have succumbed to an impulse that is less than ideal. More likely, they feel righteous in doing so: they feel they have taken a stand and done the only decent thing. They are likely to believe that some moral absolute has been violated, and that a total condemnation of the violators is an act of moral seriousness. We're seeing this play out most vividly in the aftermath of the recent US Supreme Court decision to overturn *Roe v. Wade*. Each side of that issue clearly regards its own as the only conceivable moral position, such that people on the other side are morally inferior. Not that they just have a morally inferior position, mind you – but that they are morally inferior people whose inferiority can be determined along a single axis (medieval misogynists *versus* baby murderers). No moral or human complexity is to be admitted, and no discussion is possible. One's opponents are not to be understood and then engaged, because they are not worthy of it – instead, each side sees the other as irredeemable. There is only winning and losing now.

On one level, this is understandable on an issue as deeply personal and potentially consequential as abortion. But the problem with such a feverish culture war is that victory can only ever be temporary. Each side rallies its numbers, whether in society or on the Supreme Court, and whoever wins does so by brute force. Persuasion is impossible. When more and more issues become like this, and politics becomes primarily a matter of condemning and vanquishing the opposition, a democratic society finds itself in serious trouble.

This essay argues that democracy cannot survive contempt. Democracy is about cultivating a common life even in the presence of serious disagreement. Contempt is about having no life in common at all. To make this argument requires a careful consideration of both contempt and democracy.

But it also requires us to think about the conditions in which we are going about our democratic lives. And so, we make our argument in three stages.

First, we draw on the insights of moral philosophy to make clear what we mean by contempt, and to identify precisely what makes it morally suspect. Along the way, we engage with recent philosophical and political arguments that seek to validate contempt in certain circumstances. Even those arguments, we note, require participants in public debate to practise a high level of restraint. Next, we show that such restraint is rendered completely unrealistic given the environment in which our public conversation takes place. We argue that the machinery of public discourse, dominated by media and social media, is powerfully designed to manipulate, inflame and commodify our moral emotions, impelling us towards an unrestrained contempt for each other. Finally, we argue that such contempt is ultimately incompatible with, and thoroughly corrosive of, democracy itself.

In doing this, we inevitably draw heavily on American examples. This may seem strange in an Australian essay intended largely for an Australian audience, but we do so for two reasons. The first is that since social media drives so much contemptuous public exchange, America has an oversized influence on public conversation in Australia. English-speaking social media is dominated by American ideas and trends. It is not merely that hashtags such as #MeToo and #BlackLivesMatter began in the United States and instantly went global. It is that so much of the most politically charged language – "virtue signalling" and "white male privilege"; "snowflakes" and "microaggressions" – is wholly imported from America. Moreover, Australian social-media users are subject to the same algorithms as American users, and the hostility-inducing effects of these algorithms have been demonstrated in multi-nation studies. We also know that these social media platforms are becoming increasingly influential in how Australians consume news. The internet has overtaken television as Australians' main news source, with social media driving this across every age group. Nearly a quarter of Australians use social media mostly for this purpose. And while we take comfort that the reliance on social media for news seems to have fallen slightly in the past year, that is of limited consequence if social media is significantly influencing the output of media organisations themselves. In any event, the political contagion of American politics was immediately visible in Australia after the election of Donald Trump in 2016, when everyone jostled to refract their place along the Australian political spectrum through the new president-elect. Prime Minister Malcolm Turnbull started calling the ABC's 7.30 "elite media." Opposition leader Bill Shorten proposed a crackdown on the 457 visa program and pledged to "buy Australian, build Australian, make in Australia and employ Australians." In this context, and given the enormous volume of American data available, we expect readers will see echoes of much of their own Australian experience, even if in a less intense form here, in American public discourse.

Second, of all English-speaking democracies, the United States has walked furthest down the road of contempt as a way of doing politics and public debate. It therefore provides the starkest illustrations of what a contemptuous democratic culture leaves in its wake – of just how much damage contempt can do to democracy. America's deep divisions, bordering on dysfunction, sounds an early warning to other democracies, including ours. Here, we note that Australian democracy has some naturally moderating advantages over its American counterpart. Our tradition of compulsory voting forces major parties to appeal beyond their bases. Our system of parliamentary sovereignty and our relatively modest constitution (without anything like America's bill of rights) means that the kind of stand-off we now witness between the executive branch and the Supreme Court, on matters as grave as gun control, abortion and environmental protection, simply cannot happen here. Even so, it was notable that in the days following the death of Supreme Court Justice Ruth Bader Ginsburg, op-eds appeared in Britain and Australia lamenting the absence of "hero activist" judges in those nations, rather than being grateful for the kind of quiet, moderate jurisprudence that makes activist judges unnecessary. Such is the extent to which American political culture tints Australian political lenses.

In drawing on so many instances of contempt from the United States, we do not wish to conflate Australia and the US, but to prevent them becoming more alike. Resisting contempt means resisting the influence of a social-media culture that accentuates and elevates all that is most perverse about American public discourse. What remains is for us to explain exactly why contempt is to be resisted.

WHAT IS CONTEMPT?

Humans have a vast reservoir of what are sometimes called reactive moral emotions: anger, resentment, envy, vengefulness, shame and, of course, contempt. These emotions are moral in the sense that they spring from some sense of moral wrong – from the feeling that we have been slighted, or that something we cherish has been treated with disdain. Each of these emotions may engage certain moral faculties, but not necessarily in the same way and not with unmixed results. For instance, philosophers going all the way back to Aristotle have recognised both the importance and the danger of anger as a moral emotion – one that, when properly disciplined and directed, can alert us to the presence of injustice and even help bring about restitution. Not so vengeance, which may similarly erupt in response to a moral wrong, but whose ferocity is incompatible with the requirements of proportional justice. It is common for moral philosophers to be nuanced and extremely cautious when it comes to such reactive emotions; they rarely dismiss moral emotions outright, and never simply condone them. It should tell us something, then, that until recently contempt has been almost universally condemned as the kind of moral emotion from which nothing good can come. There may be a place for anger and resentment, but rarely, if ever, for contempt.

What changed? About forty years ago, amid a renewed interest in the moral emotions among philosophers, there came a surprising reconsideration of contempt. A rehabilitation, even. Philosophers writing in this vein did not just go back to the sources and revisit Greek philosophy and tragedy or reread the treatises of Roman Stoics such as Seneca; they also drew liberally on modern literature and cinema. Michelle Mason, for instance, commences an influential essay by discussing Jean-Luc Godard's 1963 film *Le Mépris* – or, in English, *Contempt*. Based on Alberto Moravia's 1954 novel *Il disprezzo*, the film centres on the imploding marriage of a couple, Camille and Paul. Paul is a playwright, who is invited to work on a film adaptation of Homer's *Odyssey* by a wealthy American producer, Jeremiah Prokosch. Prokosch, in turn, is a lecher, and has clear sexual designs on Camille.

But so eager is Paul for the career opportunity that he is unperturbed by Prokosch's sexual advances towards his wife and might even be encouraging of them. At one point, for instance, Paul encourages Camille to ride with Prokosch, despite her hesitation, in a two-seater convertible, while Paul takes a taxi. When Paul arrives at the chalet half an hour late, blaming traffic, Camille becomes mistrustful, suspecting Paul of helping to engineer a seduction and, in Mason's summary, of "revealing himself willing to barter her sexual services for his own professional advancement." This, concludes Camille, reveals that Paul is "not a man."

"Thus begins Camille's contempt," observes Mason. Camille later makes this contempt explicit to Paul in a final confrontation, during which Paul denies Camille's charge that he effectively bartered her and offers to cut all ties with Prokosch as proof. Camille, however, is not for turning, and leaves the contemptible Paul for Prokosch.

Mason uses Camille's example as "a paradigm case" of contempt, and through it she identifies its defining elements. Camille is not merely angry at Paul. Her assessment is not that he has done wrong and hurt her, but that his unprincipled cravenness and servility renders him undeserving of the label of "a man." His is not a failure of conduct, but of essence. This lessens his worth as a person and leads Camille to rank him accordingly. Thus can Camille be said to *despise* Paul in the full sense of the Latin root *despicere*, meaning "to look down upon."

Immediately several distinguishing features of contempt become clear. The first is that contempt is *personal*. It does not condemn acts, but people as people. Accordingly, it refuses the Augustinian dictum that one should "despise the sin but not the sinner," reading whatever it regards as "sin" into the very being of the sinner. Contempt does not truly concern itself with wrongdoing, but with "badbeing," to borrow Macalester Bell's useful expression. In Mason's formulation, it regards people (or groups of people) "as being in themselves contemptible, in virtue of some quality that defines a more enduring aspect of their identity . . . The 'sin' in such a case is simply an outer manifestation of something taken to go to the core of the 'sinner'." This marks a key distinction between contempt and, say, resentment. We usually resent some fact or phenomenon about the world – "I resent the gender pay gap" – rather than a person. And as Mason notes, even when we say we resent people, we typically say we resent them *for* something, most often an act. But when we hold someone in contempt – when we contemn them – we simply name that person as an object.

So, Camille does not say Paul is not acting like a man. She says he *is not* one. But that implies some standard by which a man may be judged. It presumes a set of expectations, a series of demands we make of others and rights we claim from them. In short, there must be some set of norms: the contemnor is imposing a standard upon the contemned. This is what enables someone to look down upon another as an object that is low in rank.

But such a judgment is not sufficient for contempt. To stop here would be to stop with mere despisal or disdain. Contempt is only complete when the contemnor expresses this in some way. In Camille's case, it takes the form of deliberately allowing Paul to discover her in Prokosch's arms so she can declare her contempt for Paul and leave with Prokosch. But we could easily imagine all manner of expression, ranging from shunning to actively shaming or even inflicting violence or torture. Such action is necessary because, as Mason has it, "we feel pained in the presence of [contempt's] object, which thereby becomes for us a source of aversion." Ultimately, then, contempt is a way of acting and feeling towards another.

Taken together, we may distil the concept of contempt as follows. It is *judgmental*, in the sense that it makes categorical or totalising evaluations of people, rather than confining itself to a person's actions or particular character traits. It is *comparative*, in the sense that it deems its object to be morally inferior, which thereby confirms or even enhances the moral standing of the one showing contempt – at least in their own eyes. And it is *performative*, in the sense that it disposes us to act in certain apparent ways towards its object, which may include ridicule, humiliation, disgust or ostracism.

Contempt in practice

It is important to notice, at this point, that contempt ends up being a disposition. Anger flashes and fades, but contempt suggests something more enduring. It becomes a way of doing business with the contemned – or pointedly not doing business, as the case may be. It is something that structures and defines social relationships. It is a means of putting people in their place according to some scheme or other. We might then think of three broad kinds of contempt, connoting different social or moral schemes.

The first is what could be called patronising contempt. It is not malevolent, exactly, though entitlement and an assumed position of superiority can easily tip over into violence when that superiority is challenged. It can often find itself mixed with a certain affection and inflected with statements of appreciation or value. But in this kind of contempt, the direction of knowledge, of communication, of effective action, is only ever one way.

We see an example of this in the Turnbull government's response to the Uluru Statement from the Heart. Recall that this was the culmination of a government-commissioned process of consultation and deliberation within Indigenous Australia, as a way of discerning what form Indigenous people thought constitutional recognition should take. It was a process of extraordinary depth and breadth over six months, before an intense four-day convention at Uluru sought to distil a coherent statement from the diverse perspectives of those who had been consulted. The convention had to navigate all the impassioned disagreements and the high-stakes questions about competing notions of Indigenous and settler-state sovereignty. Some delegates walked out. But somehow, 80 per cent of delegates assented to the result, which can properly be called a *cri de coeur*, a cry of the soul seeking to reconcile the pain of dispossession with the sovereignty of the Australian parliament. Its best-known proposal was to establish a constitutionally enshrined Indigenous "Voice to Parliament." This Voice would be a standing advisory group but would have no formal power. It would not vote on, pass or block any legislation. The government's response – led by Malcolm Turnbull himself and his deputy, Barnaby Joyce – misleadingly insisted that it would be seen as a "third chamber" of parliament, declared the Australian people would never accept that, and summarily dismissed the whole idea. In short, it mischaracterised the Voice, rejected a proposal the Uluru Statement never made, and declared the matter closed without any public debate.

"Asking people what they want and then rejecting it because it doesn't align with one's poorly conceived idea of liberalism is one thing," wrote Megan Davis (herself a leader of the Uluru process) a year later. "Ignoring one of the few deliberative constitutional processes in Australia's history, particularly for a population that was excluded the first time around, is another." For Davis, this revealed "an incurable contempt for the authority and legitimacy of Aboriginal and Torres Strait Islander peoples as the first peoples of this nation." In this case, it is not that the Turnbull government assailed Indigenous people with insults. It is that it so casually dismissed the exhausting, emotionally fraught work the federal government had asked of the Indigenous deliberators. It failed to make the slightest gesture towards taking this effort and its results seriously. It bluntly refused to know Indigenous Australia, or even to hear it. That is the nature of patronising contempt: it is a form of knowing without being known; of speaking without being addressed.

A second form of contempt is more visceral. It is closer to disgust but includes a moral dimension. This is the contempt of racists, of segregationists and anti-miscegenationists. It is also, commonly, a conflation of humans with animals, with chattels, with fauna. Perhaps the quintessential instance of this is in slavery, as we see from Frederick Douglass's first-hand reflections on America's slave markets:

> Then, too, there was the intensified degradation of the spectacle. What an assemblage! Men and women, young and old, married and single; moral and intellectual beings, in open contempt of their humanity, leveled at a blow with horses, sheep, horned cattle and swine! Horses and men – cattle and women – pigs and children – all

> holding the same rank in the scale of social existence; and all subjected to the same narrow inspection, to ascertain their value in gold and silver – the only standard of worth applied by slaveholders to slaves! How vividly, at that moment, did the brutalizing power of slavery flash before me! Personality swallowed up in the sordid idea of property! Manhood lost in chattelhood!

Disgust and patronising dismissal – both of these forms might be considered examples of what William Miller calls "downward contempt." To adapt Miller, this is the contempt of adults for teenagers, men for women, masters for servants, bosses for workers, Christians for Jews, whites for blacks, the educated for the uneducated. This sort of contempt reflects (and perhaps reinforces) a hierarchical order. It does not require the contemned to do anything in particular. It requires them merely to hold a social rank, irrespective of how they got there. It assumes a rigidly hierarchical social scheme.

That is not the kind of contempt Camille has for Paul in *Le Mépris*. Camille's contempt – our third form – is moral: a form of censure, of judgment, an affirmation of one's moral superiority over another. This is the contempt of Hillary Clinton for Trump's deplorables. No pre-existing social hierarchy is necessary for this. Sure, it can be downward, but it can also be a kind of "upward" contempt, crudely defined: women for men, black for white, and so on. It is certainly the kind of contempt we are likely to encounter in the maelstrom of culture wars or the trench warfare of politics. It is a staple of the tabloid media. Think, for instance, of the perennial media condemnation of "dole bludgers," and the politics that proceeds from this: the bipartisan refusal to increase the JobSeeker payment above the poverty line; rolling "crackdowns" on welfare payments; the Morrison government's RoboDebt scandal. Indeed, RoboDebt could be a signature example of moral contempt, literally automating the judgment of people as welfare cheats (often incorrectly) and then depriving them of a human ear to which to make their case. By relegating people to the unaccountable calculation of machines in this way, the government was instituting a program of bureaucratic shunning.

Perhaps nothing better fits the definition of moral contempt than online "cancel culture," whereby someone whom internet users deem to have transgressed a sacred moral standard finds themselves at the bottom of an online pile-on, a rapid swarm of public shaming, often accompanied by calls for them to be shunned, boycotted, fired from their jobs or worse – in short, "cancelled." The contempt is embedded in the language: cancellation carries with it the sense of something being annulled, destroyed, undone, neutralised, erased or terminated; in other words, it is to delete both the thing itself and its very memory.

The idea of being "cancelled" begins, oddly enough, with the 1991 action film *New Jack City*. In it, a drug lord, played by Wesley Snipes, dumps his girlfriend with the line: "Cancel that bitch. I'll buy another one." The contemptuous overtones are obvious here: a girlfriend is an interchangeable thing you can buy. But the line would long have been forgotten were it not referenced in 2014 in an obscure reality TV show, *Love and Hip Hop: New York*, when one cast member censures his girlfriend by saying, "Get away from me. You're cancelled," and later identifies Snipes' line as his inspiration. Black Twitter found this hilarious, and the term began circulating as a joke – often as a disproportionate way of expressing disapproval of a friend over some mild disagreement: "Mike thinks 'Takeover' is Jay-Z's best song, so he's cancelled," to make up an example. The joke is in the fact that cancelling someone on such trivial grounds is a gross overreaction. But as the entropy of the internet took over, cancellation soon stopped being a joke and took its familiar form of shaming transgressors publicly – often celebrities, but also frequently and devastatingly not, as Jon Ronson has shown.

Cancellation is therefore totalising. It almost always charges its target with being guilty of some -ism or -phobia – allegations that stick to the very being or soul of a person who is thereby -ist or -phobic by nature. Accordingly, the cancelled person becomes of low rank when judged by the moral lights of the cancelling swarm, who, of course, assume a position of unassailable moral superiority. Over time, cancellation has become a kind of online disposition. As such, it meets each of the elements of our definition of contempt.

These three species or types of contempt are not mutually exclusive. Each can easily bleed into and inflect the others. Consider the now infamous example of Yassmin Abdel-Magied, hounded out of her livelihood and ultimately her country by a concerted campaign led by News Corp papers, shock-jocks and senior politicians. In a narrow sense, Abdel-Magied's "sin" was to disrespect the Anzacs by using Anzac Day to post on her Facebook page "LEST. WE. FORGET. (Manus, Nauru, Syria, Palestine ...)". But she had become a target months earlier when, appearing on the ABC's *Q&A* program, she declared in a debate with Jacqui Lambie that "Islam to me is the most feminist religion." This notion incensed the reactionary wing of Australian politics, and outlets led by *The Australian* immediately set about attacking her. By the time Anzac Day arrived, Abdel-Magied's every word was being parsed for potential controversy, which is how her Facebook post was so quickly blown out of proportion and turned into a national scandal: dozens of scathing editorials and opinion pieces, repeated front-page splashes based on screenshots of Abdel-Magied's Facebook exchanges, hundreds of articles across every major newspaper, petitions in condemnation and support with thousands of signatures. Nothing could stop the onslaught. Not even her immediate attempts to recant, when she deleted the words in brackets from her post, and wrote: "It was brought to my attention that my last post was disrespectful, and for that, I apologise unreservedly."

This was clearly a case of moral contempt, in which self-appointed defenders of Anzac and national pride decided that Abdel-Magied had committed a serious moral transgression in using the moment and language of Anzac commemoration to criticise Australia on human-rights grounds. But plenty of people express more scathing versions of that idea without censure. Abdel-Magied was surely targeted not merely for what she did, but for who she was: a Muslim woman prepared not only to defend her religion, but to do so on feminist grounds. Here, the contempt inherits at least something of the visceral "downward" kind, by tapping into prejudices against Islam, Muslims in general and Muslim women in particular.

Contempt and its discontents

The Abdel-Magied episode demonstrates something of the nature of contempt. Notice the futility of Abdel-Magied's immediate retraction and apology. Because contempt involves total condemnation of a person, it tends to contaminate the way we view each other – such that, as Mason has it, "there is a point beyond which forgiveness and reconciliation might no longer be forthcoming."

Recall in *Le Mépris* that Paul strenuously denies Camille's charge and pledges to resign from Prokosch's film as proof of his sincerity, but this makes no difference to Camille, who has already passed a final judgment on Paul himself, and therefore has no way back to him. Forgiveness requires us to separate the sin from the sinner: by refusing to do this, the contemnor "risks losing the capacity to forgive." We see this in the countless online apologies from targets of cancellation that end up being as futile as Abdel-Magied's was. Such apologies may be ignored, derided as "non-apologies," or dismissed as somehow insincere or egotistical – "making it all about yourself." Once the framework of contempt is established, once a categorical judgment is made of the object's "badbeing," any response by them is liable to be interpreted in such a reinforcing way. Contempt thus inculcates a kind of interpretive blindness.

As such, contempt by its very nature marks the end of the conversation. It is a full stop. A contemned object, as a morally inferior being, has nothing to offer, no contribution to make, no reason to be heard. Contempt is therefore what Thomas Hill Jr calls "a deep dismissal," one that terminates exchange. This is why victims of cancellation, much like Abdel-Magied, hardly have a presence in the frenzies that surround them. Their input is not particularly welcome or relevant, except to the extent it provides further fuel for the contemptuous fire already burning. Once a position of superiority is assumed in this way, the contemnor becomes unanswerable to the contemned – and publicly so – just as the Turnbull government became unanswerable to the authors of the Uluru Statement.

We see a more subtle version of this in the fashionable online phrase "educate yourself." This is typically the language of activists seeking to charge people with something like racism or sexism, but it does so by disavowing engagement altogether. Naturally, "education" is presumed to yield only one possible outcome, and that is agreement with the activist's worldview. We see this in the popular genre of online articles (inspired by the title of a bestselling book) that explain "Why I'm no longer talking to …" The assumption here is that the other's prejudice is so rank, their moral position so retrograde, or their blindness so total, that they do not deserve to be addressed. The activist is urging people to accept an argument, but disavows any obligation to persuade those who disagree, on the basis that the argument is so self-evidently right that opposition to it must be in bad faith. Certainly, that might be true of some people, and in some cases it really might be the wisest thing not to persist arguing over a stalemate. But it is altogether different to dismiss a whole class of people in this way, and to do so publicly as a kind of performative affectation. The result is a public discourse that is increasingly solipsistic, where writers give up on offering cross-cutting analyses that might cause an opponent to pause and reflect, and prefer instead to write exclusively for those who are already convinced, to give the sharpest expression to their already shared convictions, to fire up the base. Perhaps most troubling of all is that such writing is meant to signal the moral seriousness of the writer – as if the hard labour of patient appeal was somehow less morally laudable. We've witnessed across media outlets an ever-increasing number of opinion pieces whose fierce conviction and frankly contemptuous, unanswerable tone mask an underlying lack of clarity and an even more disturbing absence of hope in the moral possibilities of persuasion. One of us, in his capacity as an opinion editor, is flooded with such submissions.

Given all this, it's not hard to see why contempt has received so little support in the history of moral philosophy. The most fundamental objection comes from Immanuel Kant, for whom contempt violates two cardinal principles: the principle of human dignity and the principle of not using others as means to one's own end. Contempt violates the former because it denies the worth of the whole person, and it violates the latter because it makes another's humiliation merely the means of one's own self-aggrandisement. Central to Kant's moral vision is an idea that is central to the very concept of human rights: that humans have an inalienable dignity simply by virtue of being humans: "a worth that has no price." Contempt, meanwhile, is "[j]udging something to be worthless." It is therefore "in every case contrary to duty" because it "den[ies] them the respect owed to human beings." Kant quite specifically has the performative dimension of contempt in his sights when he says:

> At times one cannot, it is true, help inwardly looking down on some in comparison with others (*despicatui habere*); but the outward manifestation of this is, nevertheless, an offense.

Moral judgment, then, is inevitable and necessary. As Aristotle held, part of a proper moral education is developing the habits of "enjoying and hating finely," which is to say moral discernment, and even well-targeted moral censure. But, insists Kant:

> the censure of vice . . . must never break out into complete contempt and denial of any moral worth to a vicious human being; for on this supposition he could never be improved, and this is not consistent with the idea of a human being, who as such (as a moral being) can never lose entirely his predisposition to the good.

And yet, for all this, "Things are looking up for looking down on people." That's the sober assessment of philosopher David Sussman of this more recent trend in moral philosophy that seeks to recover contempt as an appropriate moral attitude. Broadly speaking, that defence takes two related forms: one theoretical, another political.

A theoretical defence of contempt

Both Michelle Mason and Macalester Bell have tried to lay out the conditions in which contempt might be deemed morally appropriate. While they acknowledge the specific dangers associated with contempt, they nonetheless maintain that a kind of totalising assessment of another person's character can be justified where that person's moral failure is so severe that it effectively overwhelms any countervailing claim of the underlying dignity of the person or insistence that they should continue to have a place within our moral community. This would be the type of moral failure that might lead us to characterise another person as a *moral monster*, or to call them, without exaggeration, a racist or a misogynist.

Such a judgment requires what could be called a hierarchy of character traits – which would mean that if certain vicious qualities can be identified in a person, they necessarily contaminate or otherwise negate whatever admirable qualities might also be present. For this to hold, the hierarchy of character traits would need to be true, and the assessment of another person's nobler qualities would need to have been done in good faith. The problem is that contempt tends to engender a jaundiced view of its object, such that we refuse to see or even acknowledge another person's virtues, or to weigh them fairly. Contempt thereby becomes self-fulfilling: at the risk of tautology, we tend to see the objects of our contempt through the prism of our judgment that they are contemptible. But for contempt's defenders, this doesn't mean contempt is always wrong, only that in practice it might often be.

Even so, this implies a rather minimalist view of the inherent dignity of human beings and the respect we owe them. Stephen Darwall offers an account of exactly this, by drawing a distinction between "recognition respect" – where we simply give appropriate weight to the fact that every other person is a human being – and "appraisal respect" – where we positively evaluate them. Recognition respect requires only that we acknowledge the moral and legal rights of those we seek to condemn; in the view of Bell and Mason, this is ultimately all we owe other human beings. In this way, they attempt to reconcile their view of contempt with Kantian notions of inalienable human dignity. Contempt is therefore properly focused only where it preserves this sort of respect.

But that leaves open to dispute precisely what moral and legal rights are owed under recognition respect. Does it confer only a minimal right to non-violence? Or a mere legal right to a presumption of innocence, but no protection from a social presumption of guilt? Does it include a right not to be deprived of one's livelihood? What about a moral right not to be publicly harassed or shamed? The answers to such questions could dramatically change the character and scope of what legitimate contempt is meant to mean.

Whatever it means, it's clear that to be justified, contempt must be heavily circumscribed. In their attempts to validate contempt, both Mason and Bell place a series of conditions on its use in light of the obvious moral objections contempt invites. While their formulations are slightly different, Bell's is a useful distillation, and a workable summary might run as follows.

The target of any legitimate contempt must actually be contemptible in the way alleged. That is, the target must be guilty of a serious moral failing and we must have good evidence of this. What counts as a serious moral failing? Broadly, Bell says it is one with "the potential to seriously impair our relationships with other persons." Later she specifies that it would include "vices of superiority" like "hypocrisy, arrogance [and] racism" but leaves room for other vices to be added.

Bell then imposes further conditions. For instance, there must not be any circumstance that excuses this moral failure, such as it being the result of, say, childhood trauma or mental illness. Additionally, the contempt cannot be hypocritical: the contemnor must "actually care about the standard or fault in question." Finally, any judgment that someone is worthy of contempt must be provisional. The one showing contempt must not be "utterly unresponsive to reasons that count in favor of overcoming his contempt through a process of forgiveness."

To illustrate how this might work, Bell has recourse to literature – in this case Jane Austen's *Pride and Prejudice*. She presents the example of Elizabeth Bennet's rejection of Mr Darcy's marriage proposal. Elizabeth regards Darcy as a pompous, callous, uncaring snob – that is, she holds him guilty of several vices of superiority – and accordingly holds him in contempt. When Darcy proposes to her, Elizabeth rejects him in a contemptuous way, lacerating him for his arrogance and treatment of others. This wounds his pride and shocks him into recognising his moral faults. He writes a letter to Elizabeth giving some account of himself, and Elizabeth herself relents. Of this process Darcy exclaims: "What do I not owe you! You taught me a lesson, hard indeed at first, but most advantageous. By you, I was properly humbled." A conspicuous theme of Darcy's development throughout the novel is his declining level of prejudice, of vices of superiority.

Here, Elizabeth Bennet's contempt operates as an act of moral communication. It is appropriate because it enhances, rather than impairs, her relationship with Darcy. It is the means by which she alerts Darcy to his arrogance and corrects the imbalanced status of their relationship. By looking down on the one who routinely looks down on others (including her), she helps him "appreciate the reasons he has to change his ways."

But an epistemological objection immediately arises at this point. Even this restricted form of contempt requires us to make judgments of people that extend well beyond what is knowable to human beings. Even if we were to conclude – *contra* Kant – that a human can be sufficiently rotten to be worthy of contempt, that can only be justified where our assessment of that rottenness is correct. But if that assessment must also take account of any ameliorating or extenuating circumstances in that person's life or background, a just assessment requires a truly mighty level of knowledge. It requires us to sit in something akin to divine judgment on what Jean Hampton calls a person's "inner moral state" – a near impossible task even in respect of our own selves, much less someone else.

We might even use Bell's example from *Pride and Prejudice* to make this point. The thing about Elizabeth Bennet's appraisal of Darcy is that she's actually mistaken. When Darcy explains himself in his letter to Elizabeth, she realises not only that she is mistaken, but also that she is guilty of a similar prejudice to that with which she charges Darcy. In one of the inner monologues that Jane Austen regularly gives her characters, Elizabeth says that Darcy's letter "overthrows" her certain knowledge of his character, his motives and conduct. She acknowledges that she herself had been "blind, partial, prejudiced, absurd"; and finally reflects that, "Till this moment, I never knew myself." There is no doubt that this is a communicative episode, but it is only constructive because Darcy responded constructively to it. And part of the reason for that is surely that he was already in love with Elizabeth. Darcy has every incentive to react constructively because he ultimately wants to win her love. In short, things work out precisely because Darcy isn't contemptuous of Elizabeth, as she was of him. He finds her response difficult to take, but ultimately does so in good faith because the relationship already has some level of familiarity or affection (even if not requited) on which to draw. But the details of the story furnish a warning: even with that familiarity, Elizabeth's moral judgment of Darcy is false, and therefore in some sense unjust.

We can lower the required standard of knowledge for contemptuous judgment if we like, but the more we do, the shakier contempt's moral claims become. That is especially true of the kind of public shaming which occurs when those exhibiting contempt can have no such knowledge of the one being contemned – certainly nothing like the familiarity Elizabeth has with Darcy. The target may be a public figure known only in the caricatured form of news coverage or popular culture, or some hitherto anonymous private citizen about whom we know nothing beyond their sudden appearance in a public controversy.

The political implications of Bell's defence of contempt are obvious. Bell sees Elizabeth Bennet's contempt as legitimate because it turns the tables on Darcy. Here, contempt becomes a kind of equalising disposition. This is the thread that political arguments for contempt tend to pick up, along the following lines.

Contempt as political virtue

Contempt of those one regards as being beneath oneself has long been one of the luxuries of a certain social or political rank – obviously of class, but also of race and gender. Accordingly, in one view this "downward" contempt is best met not by indifference or silent loathing, much less by self-defeated acquiescence, but by a kind of countervailing affect. A "hot" emotion like resentment or indignation may not be the best option, however, because it threatens to consume the contemned, and to be met with either indifference or a perverse satisfaction by the contemnor, who is then confirmed in a position of social, and even moral, superiority. More effective, so the argument goes, is "upward" contempt – or a kind of counter-contempt – whereby the arrogance of the contemnor is met with scorn, ridicule, disdain. This expresses a refusal to grant the contemnor any moral sanction, and issues a stern moral judgment of one's own.

At this point, the question becomes not whether contempt is legitimate, but whether it might in fact be virtuous. In Michelle Mason's terms, the question is "whether such contempt is not merely morally justifiable but, perhaps, morally required in certain circumstances." Contempt becomes a mode of moral seriousness, much like anger, but also politically useful and constructive. This should be especially so within democratic societies, which, unlike hierarchical societies, are at least normatively egalitarian. For, as William Miller insists, democracies "arm the lower with some of the contempts that only the high had available to them before." Indeed, he goes on, "[i]t might just be that the mutuality of contempt is much of what pluralistic democracy is all about." In this vision, the civic equality of democracy does not reduce the conditions for contempt. Rather, it binds us in mutual contempt: "Every person is now entitled to think his vote undervalued in comparison with those of all those contemptible others with whom democracy has lumped him."

This political reassessment of contempt needs to be taken seriously, because it compels us to acknowledge something important about the classical refusal of contempt: that it often silenced the contemned. Consider, for instance, the transitional role that contempt played in the late-eighteenth and nineteenth centuries when it came to deflating the pretentions and incestuous self-regard of the aristocratic and land-owning classes, particularly in the form of satire or public ridicule.

We will return to consider this more fully later. For now, it is sufficient to note an obvious concern. Vices such as hypocrisy, arrogance and racism are broad categories, and in many cases are being defined ever more broadly and in ever more contested ways. As Amy Chua observes of "cultural appropriation," on which charges of racism are frequently now based:

> Not long ago, it was considered left wing and a sign of multicultural openness – a rejection of ethnocentrism – for a Caucasian person to wear a sari or a kimono, or to sport cornrows or dreadlocks. Today any of these acts might be considered a "microagression," a transgression of group boundaries by members of a dominant group.

One response to this might be to say that the definition of a transgression is entirely in the eye of the beholder. So, for instance, it doesn't matter how broadly or even idiosyncratically someone wants to define racism; as long as something meets that person's sincere definition, contempt can be valid. But that would overlook something about personal ideals that Michelle Mason concedes: the fact that they "are subject to deformation and excess" and might even become so high or broad that they become unrealistic. She continues: "In holding others (and ourselves) up to unrealistic standards we risk finding fault where none ought to be ascribed." This is a particular risk in the online world, where so many such accusations are hurled, because, as one American study has shown, the most extreme, aggressive and least representative political voices on either side of the political divide dominate political debate. Accordingly, the ideals and definitions of vice by which people are contemned are likely to be ones the mainstream population considers flawed, fringe or overly pure. Moreover, since people gain status in online debates through this condemnation of others, there is an incentive to make these ideals ever more unrealistic. Many people therefore quickly go from being active participants in a pile-on to being victims of one when they fail to live up to the relevant standard. An example might be Michelle Law, who led an online campaign against the Sydney Film Festival for giving an award to the film *Mukbang*, which she and others deemed racist on cultural appropriation grounds, only to issue an apology of her own within a month when someone unearthed a scene from one of her own films and levelled the same charge at her.

We therefore remain sceptical of Bell's and Mason's efforts to formulate a more judicious version of contempt, especially once we consider what it means for democratic politics. If we are to adopt the kind of conditions on contempt that Bell and Mason propose, we must ask to what extent they make sense in a public setting. This takes us well beyond the world of Camille, Paul and *Le Mépris*, and beyond the world of Elizabeth Bennet and Mr Darcy in *Pride and Prejudice*. Indeed, it takes us beyond the world of any number of hypothetical scenarios through which moral principles are so often teased out in works of moral philosophy. It requires us to consider not merely the isolated principles of valid contempt – political or otherwise – but the environment in which those principles would need to be enacted. Put bluntly, is the kind of "fitting" contempt we encounter in modern moral philosophy realistic in the public sphere of modern democracy? For any way you approach contempt – and whatever species of it you wish to consider – there is always one thing that is true: contempt is not simply felt; it is communicated. It is a form of communication meant to wither, to censure, to reduce. And, like hate speech or even satire, it cannot form part of the public sphere without changing the "air" between citizens. We must therefore consider the nature of that air.

AIR QUALITY: THE CONDITIONS OF OUR COMMON LIFE

"I can't breathe." When George Floyd desperately uttered these words – no fewer than twenty-seven times – as he lay prone with Derek Chauvin's knee pressing down on the back of his neck, he was being shockingly literal. But when his words became the defining slogan of a protest movement against police brutalisation of black bodies, they became something altogether more comprehensive: a metaphor for the suffocating reality of so much black life in America, with the threat of unpunished police violence hanging so heavily in the air. Indeed, Floyd's words were a reprise of so many others' dying words – Javier Ambler II in Austin, Texas; Manuel Ellis in Tacoma, Washington; David Dungay Jr in New South Wales – and Floyd's murder is not even where the phrase's widespread use as a protest slogan began. That was six years prior, when Eric Garner said it eleven times in the chokehold of one New York City police officer, while another pushed his head hard against the pavement and at least two others placed their combined weight on his back. Not only would there be no homicide convictions for this violence, there would be no indictment. Hence the telling response of George Floyd's brother, Philonise, when Derek Chauvin was finally convicted: "Today we are able to breathe again."

"Air is the medium of our natural and spiritual life, of our relation to ourselves, to speaking, to the other." So often we use "air" as French philosopher Luce Irigaray has done here: as a symbol of our common life. It is that thing that occupies the space between us, that we inhale in common, and on which we are therefore mutually dependent. Perhaps Hannah Arendt has it best when she describes the earth's atmosphere as the "quintessence of the human condition," that which makes breath and movement, speech and action, deliberation and co-operation possible "without artifice." For Arendt, air is what allows us to make meaning out of our shared activities and pursuits, to work within and negotiate the inherent limitations of human life. The air is therefore inescapably social, and therefore ultimately political.

Hence the proliferation of air metaphors that describe our social lives. We "air" our grievances. We share moments of excitement when "the air is thick with anticipation," and moments of disappointment which "suck the air out of the room." When we disappear from the view of others, we "vanish into thin air," but find ourselves "out in the open air" when we are conspicuously public. We celebrate those who offer something new and useful as "a breath of fresh air," but deride those whose pronouncements are "full of hot air." Having so derided them, we might then need to "clear the air."

Clear the air. The metaphor implies that our common life is something to be tended, that under certain conditions it might come to be polluted to the detriment of all. "We do not breathe well. There is infamy in the air." So said Ralph Waldo Emerson on the issue of American slavery in 1851. Such infamy was so pungent that even those with no interest in politics – "who snuff oppression and dishonor at a distance" – were discomforted by the smell. The air can become so corrupted by the unheeded proliferation of social vices, such as vanity, egotism, callousness, contemptuousness, inattentiveness, thoughtlessness, deceitfulness, distrustfulness, vengefulness, cruelty, injustice and intimidation, that it becomes, in effect, unbreathable for others. A similar idea is at work in the way Jeremy Waldron characterises hate speech as posing "something like an environmental threat to social peace"; or the way Sissela Bok insists that, "*Whatever* matters to human beings, trust is the atmosphere in which it thrives."

The broad point is that our public life is beholden in some sense to the quality of the air we breathe together. If it is to remain morally habitable for human beings, the air between us must be kept healthy. And while we could never exhaustively list the factors that contribute to this, we can very easily identify some of the prime determinants – those things with an oversized influence on what we might call the social temperature, the atmospheric conditions in which we relate. The most obvious of these, and the most directly related to the topic of this essay, are our forums for public debate: media and social media. It is not for nothing that we describe a radio or television broadcast – that most expansive public square – as being "on the air," or that the signal itself is called "the airwaves."

Here, there can hardly be any doubt: the media machine is making us angry. Many of us might enjoy the odd online foray into the pleasures of gossip and inane trivia, of sugar-hit memes and heart-warming stories of human resilience – but anger is the main game. It's what seizes our attention, keeps us engaged and ultimately keeps us coming back for more. "The more anger [people] get exposed to, the more they interact and the more they consume," explained Frances Haugen, an algorithm design expert who blew the whistle on her former employer, Facebook.

This is the commodification of emotion. And that is not entirely new. Long before social media platforms insinuated themselves into our every waking moment, before the proliferation of cable news channels, before television and even the wireless, newspapers had shown themselves only too willing to excite and then exploit the passions of their audience if it meant increasing market share. We see this clearly in the rivalry between the great mass-circulation tabloids of America's "Gilded Age." And that story is, for our purposes, a particularly instructive one.

The *commodification of emotion*

By the early 1890s, Joseph Pulitzer – after whom the journalism award is named – enjoyed untrammelled dominance as the proprietor of the city's most-read paper, the *New York World*. By contrast, William Randolph Hearst was relatively new to the newspaper game, having only recently taken control of his father's newspaper, *The San Francisco Examiner*. But Hearst had dreams of a news empire that would span the entire country, and he knew that was impossible without a big presence in New York. So he moved there to take on Pulitzer, and bought the *New York Journal*.

Hearst was notorious even then for his rapacity, vulgarity and utter lack of principle. Pulitzer, for his part, was hardly immaculate. The *World*'s rapid growth under him owed much to a distinctive combination of scandal-mongering and a brand of heavily embellished storytelling that was formally closer to the lurid tales of Edgar Allan Poe or the breathy melodrama of Louisa May Alcott than to anything that appeared in the beleaguered *New York Times*. And yet, for all that, Pulitzer still considered himself a "newsman." The walls of the *World*'s city office were adorned with posters that read: "Accuracy, Accuracy, Accuracy! Who? What? Where? When? How? The Facts – The Color – The Facts!" Not so Hearst, who sought to emulate Pulitzer's successful formula, but with none of his editorial scruples.

Over the space of a few years, the fierce competition between the press barons sparked a number of changes to the way "the news" was done, perhaps the most obvious of which was the creation of the "front page," complete with larger type, three-column banner headlines and abundant line-cut illustrations. But the real innovation born of their rivalry did not simply change the appearance of the news; it was to redefine what counts as "news" in the first place. Buyers of Pulitzer's *World* and Hearst's *New York Journal* would continue to find in their pages whatever could be dredged up from the city's "sewers and morgue fields" (as one of Pulitzer's detractors put it). But market realities forced the papers to the recognition that voyeurism can only get you so far. Readers, they discovered, don't just want to be titillated or shocked. They want to be enlisted. They want their patronage of the papers to be in the service of the struggle of "good" against "evil." And the most effective way of consolidating an inconstant and disparate readership was to direct their anger against a common enemy.

So the tabloids adopted a tone that grew increasingly strident. They railed against the purveyors of corruption and the cosseted elite. They charged their political foes with nothing less than outright treachery. They printed fiery denunciations of living conditions in the tenements and working conditions at the sweatshops. They coupled graphic descriptions of homicide with broadsides on the ineptitude of the police, and would then round it all off with recklessly vigilantist calls for "citizen detectives" to solve crimes the police evidently could not, often with the offer of a sizeable reward. They printed overblown predictions of a coming "Yellow Plague," dabbled in racist innuendo and indulged in brazen jingoism. Then they would turn around and appeal to the largely untapped market of predominantly European immigrants. Sometimes, this entailed the publication of more illustrations and cartoons, for example, or uncomplicated stories in simpler English; other times, it meant pandering to the nationalist fervour or latent ethnic hostilities that many immigrants brought with them to their new country. Editorially, either was permitted if it would afford some competitive edge.

The rivalry reached its lowest point with the tabloids' reporting of the Spanish–American War. Each newspaper was determined to outdo the other when it came to whipping up public support for American intervention in Cuba, because of the boost any such war would deliver to circulation. They sent journalists and artists to the Caribbean, not so much to report on the conflict as to commodify it; to turn it into a spectacle for domestic consumption. According to an infamous anecdote (possibly apocryphal), when one of his illustrators expressed doubt that war between the United States and Spain was imminent, Hearst telegrammed back: "Please remain. You furnish the pictures, and I'll furnish the war." Knowing what their readers wanted, the tabloids applied the same sensationalist formula to the conflict in Cuba as they had long done to crime reporting in New York City – replete with the same lurid details and superficial explanations, all designed to excite public interest and incite moral outrage. As Hearst's biographer, William Swanberg, writes:

> The majority of the public found it more exciting to read about the murder of Cuban babies and the rape of Cuban women by the Spaniards than to read conscientious accounts of complicated political problems and injustices on both sides. The hero-villain concept of war was simple, easy to grasp and satisfying.

The decisive moment came in February 1898, when the USS *Maine* exploded in Havana harbour, killing 268 American sailors aboard. The *World* and the *Journal* both published the contents of a cable purportedly sent by the captain of the warship, which suggested that the explosion had been no accident. The papers raced to pronounce the tragedy "the work of the enemy," the result of "Spanish treachery." Hearst, never one to be outdone, offered a $50,000 reward for the "detection of the Perpetrator of the Maine Outrage." Readers demanded retribution.

The cable, of course, was a hoax. The explosion was an accident. The public thirst for retribution had everything to do with the story it had literally been sold, but it had nothing to do with the facts. Soon enough, Congress declared war on Spain. The newspapers had their war, and revenue went through the roof.

It would be fair to say that the contest between these turn-of-the-century tabloids ended up debasing them both. For the *Journal* and the *World* were bound by the same logic: the commercial imperative that reduces "the news" to whatever can attract and hold the attention of the most readers. Hearst may have been typically crass in his reasoning that "the public is even more fond of entertainment than it is of information," but Pulitzer was hardly more discreet when proffering why he was intent on his paper being read by "the largest number of people": because "circulation means advertising, and advertising means money, and money means independence."

Both men inherited the logic of the so-called "penny papers" of the 1830s, which first promulgated the corrupting notion that newspapers should not principally be in the business of selling news to readers, but of selling readers to advertisers. In this scheme, the "news" functions as little more than a lure, dangled before the noses of prospective buyers in the hope that it might catch their eye and entice them to part with their penny. Pulitzer and Hearst merely perfected this model. They demonstrated the fabulous success that newspapers could enjoy if only they were prepared to devalue "the news" enough – and their acolytes in the twentieth and twenty-first centuries have been panting after that success ever since.

It probably seems strange to have digressed into this brief account of the strategies of nineteenth-century American tabloids, whose model of distribution was entirely reliant on steam-powered printing presses and newsies calling out on the street corner. This seems a far cry from our digital era of unconstrained mass publication and instantaneous distribution, which has saturated our lives with words and images in a manner and to a degree that would have been unimaginable just a generation ago. And yet, no technological advancement changes what made Hearst and Pulitzer so successful: their profound insight into human nature. They understood that certain emotions are irresistible to us, and therefore ripe for exploitation. Chief among these are the moral emotions we've been discussing – emotions like anger, resentment, envy, haughtiness, self-righteousness, disdain and, yes, contempt. We are apt to buy whatever sets these emotions aflame, then go back for more and more fuel. Those emotions, those vulnerabilities, are the important aspect, not the mechanisms by which they are exploited. Technological advances such as social media merely provide a rapid, ubiquitous, updated mechanism.

The fact that social media commodifies these same emotions is now firmly established. The critical turning point came around 2009, when Facebook introduced its "Like" button, delivering users the rush and despair of having their posts scored in this way, and delivering Facebook torrents of data on users' preferences and the sorts of posts that attracted the most engagement. This pairing of data and emotion allowed Facebook to develop the algorithms that gave users the kind of content they would most "Like," and they inevitably spent more and more time on the site. Later the same year, Twitter introduced its "Retweet" function, allowing users to pass on others' tweets to their followers with a couple of clicks, when it previously required a laborious process of copying, pasting and typing out "RT" next to the original tweeter's handle. Once this process became frictionless, the potential reach of any given tweet, and the amount of people's time and attention it could occupy, expanded exponentially. Three years later, Facebook copied the idea, adding its mobile "Share" button. The most fundamental mechanism of virality was complete.

And what was likely to go viral? Twitter's answer came in 2014 with what became known as "Gamergate": a misogynist online harassment campaign of women in the video game industry. The campaign was organised on the dingy message boards of 4Chan and Reddit, but the rape threats and death threats happened in the open air of Twitter. And the Retweet button made it possible. Technologist Andy Baio analysed more than 300,000 Gamergate tweets posted in a 72-hour period and found that 69 per cent of them were retweets. Of the rest, the overwhelming majority were either not directed at anyone in particular or were direct replies to another user and therefore not fully public. Only 4 per cent of Gamergate tweets both mentioned another user publicly and were not retweets.

This more or less summarises what plenty of studies of virality have found ever since. In 2016, a New York University study discovered that in the case of moral and political content, "moral emotion is the key" for virality – a process the authors called "moral contagion." By 2021, research had refined this to a more troubling conclusion: easily the greatest predictor of virality was "out-group animosity." For perspective, moral-emotional language increased the likelihood of news items being shared and retweeted by 10 to 17 per cent. Out-group language increased it by 67 per cent. Put simply, if you want to go viral, even as a journalist, pick a side and publish nasty things about "the enemy." And whatever you do, don't use positive language: that *decreased* shares and retweets by between 2 and 11 per cent.

So, we know hostile political discussions are prime viral content. Now, thanks to the research of political scientists Alexander Bor and Michael Bang Petersen, we also know that those same discussions are driven by "status-driven individuals who are drawn to politics and are equally hostile both online and offline," and who have a much greater presence online than they do offline. Consider the overall picture that emerges. Online discussion is significantly more hostile than its offline counterpart, and dominated by unusually aggressive, hyper-political people. The rules of virality suit these people because the content most likely to be shared is impassioned, nasty and tribal, identifying and attacking political enemies. And these people do it because they are seeking status. News stories thereby become mere props in the online pageant of quasi-moral posturing and self-promotion. Meanwhile, the more reflective are comparatively silent, and their posts are very unlikely to go viral. The logic of social media perpetuates what we might call *the virality of evil*. Or, in the milder language of one of these studies, "The design structure of social media platforms may be creating perverse incentives for polarizing content when users do not truly want this."

"It is very common for humans to develop things with the best of intentions and for them to have unintended, negative consequences." These are the words of Justin Rosenstein, the former Facebook engineer who developed the Like button. Rosenstein told *The Guardian* that his aim was to allow users to "send little bits of positivity," but what it gave them instead was "bright dings of pseudo-pleasure" and a phone addiction. Now he has regrets, and an iPhone with a parental-control feature that prevents him from downloading any apps. He finds a kindred soul in Chris Wetherell, who developed Twitter's Retweet button in the belief it would amplify the voices of underrepresented communities. As he watched Gamergate unfold, Wetherell realised what he'd done. "Retweeting helped [users] get a false picture of a person out there faster than they could respond," he told *Buzzfeed*. "We didn't build a defence for that. We only built an offensive conduit." The implications soon became clear: "It dawned on me that this was not some small subset of people acting aberrantly. This might be how people behave. And that scared me to death." Hence, Wetherell's memorable lament: "We might have just handed a 4-year-old a loaded weapon."

Neither of these men intended their work to yield these consequences. But the media machine is now built, and much like Hearst and Pulitzer before them, the commercial behemoths that run it are unlikely to sacrifice what makes it profitable. It's not that every one of their innovations is nefarious. It's that the innovations that turn out that way are the ones they retain, subject only to occasional tinkering. When Frances Haugen leaked "The Facebook Files" from Facebook HQ to *The Wall Street Journal*, she merely confirmed what any remotely interested observer had already surmised: that Facebook fully knows the rapacious effects of its algorithms on individuals and on society, but that it routinely overlooks or downplays this for commercial reasons. Haugen's clearest example is the "Family and Friends" algorithm update in 2018, which prioritised posts by users' close contacts and was ostensibly designed to reduce angst. In the event, it had the opposite effect, making users angrier, and when Facebook staff sounded the alarm, Mark Zuckerberg resisted some of their suggested solutions precisely because he worried they would cause people to use Facebook less. Haugen summarised the problem neatly in an interview with America's *60 Minutes*:

> The thing I saw at Facebook over and over again was there were conflicts of interest between what was good for the public and what was good for Facebook. And Facebook, over and over again, chose to optimize for its own interests, like making more money.

The irresistible conclusion is that social media has little interest in tending to the "air." It seeks only to monetise it, even if that is best done by infusing it with toxins and hallucinogens. We know, for instance, thanks to an analysis in *Science*, that lies spread more quickly than truth on Twitter in every category of information – but that this is especially pronounced for political content. In our age, the town hall of the newspaper has given way to the individually curated social media feed – which is to say, the public square has become privatised and personalised, then set alight. The alienation of members of society from each other surely follows, not as a coincidental choice of millions of different people but as a structural feature of the way we perceive the world. The inevitable result is that we are not merely siloed by class, background or experience, but by *epistemology*. Here we witness the fulfilment of the philosopher Bernard Williams' prediction of the epistemic damage the internet would do; the ways in which it would undermine the very idea of shared knowledge. It is worth reproducing in full:

> the Internet shows signs of creating for the first time what Marshall McLuhan prophesied as a consequence of television, a global village, something that has the disadvantages both of globalization and of a village. Certainly it does offer some reliable sources of information for those who want it and know what they are looking for, but equally it supports that mainstay of all villages, gossip. It constructs

> proliferating meeting places for the free and unstructured exchange of messages which bear a variety of claims, fancies, and suspicions, entertaining, superstitious, scandalous, or malign. The chances that many of these messages will be true are low, and the probability that the system itself will help anyone to pick out the true ones is even lower. In this respect, post-modern technology may have returned us dialectically to a transmuted version of the pre-modern world, and the chances of acquiring true beliefs by these means, except for those who already have knowledge to guide them, will be much like those in the Middle Ages. At the same time, the global nature of these conversations makes the situation worse than in a village, where at least you might encounter and perhaps be forced to listen to some people who had different opinions and obsessions. As critics concerned for the future of democratic discussion have pointed out, the Internet makes it easy for large numbers of previously isolated extremists to find each other and talk only among themselves.

This has obvious, profound implications for any consideration of contempt. As we have seen, one of contempt's chief moral problems is that it presumes we can sit in quasi-divine judgment on one another. Hence the philosophical attempts to defend contempt have imposed serious requirements of evidence, openness to contrary evidence, restraint, and a certain diligence and balance in forming moral judgment of a person. But how can this be observed in public debate when the engine of social media undermines every aspect of it in a statistically demonstrable way? How do restraint and balance survive a system where deemed offences are elevated to the level of a general character trait almost instantly? Michael Lynch calls social media "an outrage factory." Siva Vaidhyanathan calls it, among other things, "an anger machine." But the research reveals both descriptions to be insufficient. For it does not merely exhort us to anger or outrage, but to moral superiority, status-seeking and a swift, deep dismissal of our designated enemies. Might we better think of it as a contempt machine?

The tabloidisation of everything

What, then, of traditional or legacy media? Even in the age of Hearst and Pulitzer, there were newspapers that believed their role was to strengthen the conditions of democratic life and build up the capacity for public deliberation. It was an optimistic idea, redolent of Alexis de Tocqueville's sense that America's proliferation of newspapers indicated an inchoate longing on the part of citizens to discover others of like mind. The newspaper was a forum, much like the Athenian *agora*, that permitted genuine deliberation and cooperative action – which is to say, democratic self-government. So, citizens who "cannot identify one another and have no idea how to meet … will meet at last and join forces," as the newspapers made visible to them the ideas they share. They could "converse every day without seeing one another and … proceed in concert without meeting."

Such a goal necessarily constrains the means newspapers should be prepared to employ. It is no wonder that *The New York Times*, whose existence was under continual threat during the Pulitzer-Hearst years, refused to succumb to the tabloids' formula for mass-circulation. Under publisher Adolph Ochs, the *Times* decided to match the penny price tag of the other papers in order to remain in the game, and it went to some lengths to elevate the appearance of its pages and the breadth of its coverage. It continued to make entreaties to prospective advertisers but refused to peddle "scandal" and "filth" or resort to partisan point-scoring, instead reiterating its pledge to "give the news impartially, without fear or favor, regardless of party, sect or interests involved." The *Times*' famous slogan – "All the News That's Fit to Print" – first appeared on the front page in February 1897. Given the timing, it must surely have been a rebuke to Hearst and Pulitzer.

Elsewhere, and especially in Australia, that high-minded sense of journalism as a vocation rather than a business has its most tangible expression in public broadcasting. The ABC, established in 1932, was a direct copy of the BBC, established ten years earlier, and both represented an overt repudiation of the worst inclinations of the tabloids. Lord John Reith acknowledged that it would have been relatively easy for the BBC to become little more than a publicly funded "clearing-house for sensationalism," but nevertheless held that "our responsibility is to carry into the greatest possible number of homes everything that is best in every department of human knowledge, endeavour and achievement, and to avoid the things which are, or may be, hurtful" – an example that the ABC would set out to follow. So, while Australia certainly has its tabloid traditions, it has inherited a media ecology from Britain that ameliorates some of their worst tendencies, leading to a rather uneasy mix of public broadcasting and advertiser-dependent broadsheets more in the tradition of *The New York Times* than the *World* or the *New York Journal*. Might that not stand as a bulwark against the depredations of social media?

To some extent, perhaps. Any account of journalism's moral calling may feel increasingly quaint, but there are still plenty of journalists and editors who believe in some version of it. The trouble is that media organisations – even those of the highest quality – are undermining their conviction. In the past two decades the media have almost entirely outsourced the distribution of content to social media platforms, which as we have seen are quite prepared to sacrifice the conditions of democratic life on the altar of profitability. News outlets have created Facebook pages and Twitter accounts, posting selections of their digital content to those pages and encouraging people to share, retweet and comment. Some mastheads even display share and retweet statistics at the top of their articles online, somewhere just beneath the byline. So even if you were visiting those sites directly, rather than through a social media link, you could read, say, an opinion piece, and know immediately how "hot" it was, according to a digital scorecard.

A charitable reading would be that news outlets feel they have little choice, and journalists have a responsibility to put their content where people will see it – which in this age is on social media platforms. A less charitable reading might say that the outlets simply couldn't resist the promise of exponentially greater "reach," of having their content in front of people who would otherwise never have found it, including people on other continents – in short, the promise of virality. Whichever reading you prefer, a pact has been struck. Social media companies benefit from having news content on their sites, which adds gravitas and legitimacy to the enterprise and (more importantly) is often very "shareable," which means people spend more time scrolling. In turn, news companies benefit from a free mass-distribution network beyond anything they could have assembled themselves.

It was therefore disingenuous in February 2021 – as the Morrison government was trying to force tech companies to pay for the news content on their sites – when media companies accused tech companies of "stealing" this content. There was no theft taking place, for the very simple reason that big media companies were willingly giving over their content: they were the ones uploading and encouraging their audiences to share it, not Facebook. They were the ones that incorporated social media into their metrics for success. They were the ones repurposing their content to optimise its shareability: clipping up the most heightened moments of the show; writing headlines using words proven to attract social media shares or which are pure clickbait. They were the ones monitoring and promoting hashtags in the hope that they might inspire "engagement" and perhaps even start "trending." This is not aberrant, unrepresentative behaviour. It is now conventional. To make the economics of the attention economy work, media outlets require audience numbers that are exponentially greater than they ever needed in the pre-digital world. Hence the observation of British journalist and academic Emily Bell that "going viral is a goal in nearly all newsrooms."

The relentless logic of this new environment means that institutionally prudent, non-partisan, non-profit broadcasters such as the ABC and the BBC, as well as editorially serious legacy media companies, including *The New York Times*, *The Atlantic*, *The Times* of London, *The Guardian* and *The Washington Post*, must compete for attention in the same market, and according to the same rules, as Fox, *Vox*, Sky, *Vice*, *BuzzFeed* and the *Daily Mail*. In recent years, we have seen some quality news outlets attempt to break free of this trend, placing less emphasis on social media metrics and more on a subscriber-based model that prizes quality over virality. We're witnessing more journalists pay less attention to platforms such as Twitter, or even abandon them altogether. We don't know how successful this fledgling approach will be, but it has a long way to go if it is to undo the effects of the last decade or so, during which the competition for web traffic among newspapers has, to varying degrees, debased them all – conspiring to make media overall louder, faster, angrier, more contemptuous, more partisan.

As a result, what might be called the "tabloid model" of mixing what is ostensibly a public service with wanton profiteering has gone from being one media model among many to the governing model of the media as a whole. This has led to what Emily Bell calls "the tabloidisation of everything." Which is to say, our informational environment has reverted to that of the Gilded Age. If one needs further demonstration of this point, consider the following lament from a former editor of *The New Republic*:

> To survive, media companies lost track of their values. Even journalists of the highest integrity have internalized a new mind-set; they worry about how to successfully pander to Google's and Facebook's algorithms. In pursuit of clicks, some of our nation's most important purveyors of news have embraced sensationalism; they have published dubious stories; they have heaped attention on propagandists and conspiracists, one of whom was elected president of the United States.

The tabloidisation of everything means a pervasive commodification of emotion. From social media in the form of algorithms, and from traditional media in service to the same. But that raises obvious questions: what, exactly, is the benefit in inciting these morally inflected emotions? And what is the effect of having something in the air that constantly inflames them?

Pulitzer and Hearst's fundamental insight was that readers needed not just titillation, but a shared task, and moral emotions provide this.

But their lesson is that these emotions can be marshalled to opposing ends. The moral outrage inspired by the press could kickstart a grass-roots campaign to boycott certain products until working conditions in the sweatshops that manufactured them are improved. Deep-seated anger towards politicians could be placed at the service of improving democratic transparency and accountability. But these emotions can just as easily be directed against purported traitors within and enemies without if that's what the unassailable laws of mass circulation demand. Or, as is increasingly the case in our social-media-saturated age, they can be given no direction at all. Instead, they can simply be allowed to turn inwards and metastasise into a kind of nihilistic disdain for one another, a stance that shows less interest in working together to improve the conditions of our common life than in tweeting insults at those with whom we disagree for the gratification and admiration of those with whom we agree.

That is the air we breathe.

It is in this atmosphere, this air, that any defence of contempt must be assessed. Contempt takes place now in an environment where emotion is commodified and exploited for profit, where powerful algorithms manipulate human psychology in order to mine it, and where media organisations, their business models under threat, find it more feasible to swim with the tide than to resist it. These are, of course, generalisations. There will be valiant efforts from citizens, politicians and journalists to buck these trends. But the trends are clear and entrenched, giving rise to dynamics of social hostility that reproduce themselves.

"One of the things we know from social psychology is when people feel threatened, they can't change, they can't listen," observed Stanford University's Alana Conner to *Vox*. What happens, then, when we rush to threaten each other with contempt? The only response we are entitled to expect is one of hardened defiance. There's no doubt, for instance, that Donald Trump's approach to politics was contemptuous toward Mexicans, Muslims and women, among others. People within these groups no doubt felt threatened, and this sense of threat will have added to their urgent desire to condemn his followers as irredeemable deplorables. But aren't we also bound to recognise the same sense of threat, of being demeaned, expressed by those who voted for Trump? As one such voter told *The Atlantic*: "maybe I'm just so sick of being called a bigot that my anger at the authoritarian left has pushed me to support this seriously flawed man."

This cycle is one reason it is more accurate to say that the air is heavy with contempt, rather than with anger. Over time – and not very much time – it becomes a standard way of doing things. It becomes habitual. Which is to say, it becomes a disposition. The models of appropriate contempt offered by Bell and Mason, with the requirements of restraint, balance and epistemic caution, seem completely unrealisable in this environment, especially at the level of politics and society. Such restraint requires deep breaths in fetid air.

This raises serious problems for the argument, sketched earlier in this essay, in favour of "upward" contempt as a way of doing politics. In an environment in which everyone claims to be victimised, "upwardness" becomes far from straightforward. Indeed, almost everyone wielding contempt would regard themselves as doing so in some upward way. Racial, gender and sexuality-based minorities, obviously. But recall that some two-thirds of working-class white people in America consider discrimination against them to be just as big a problem as discrimination against non-whites. That makes no sense whatsoever among those who understand the lives of these people along the single axis of race, in which they enjoy the untrammelled accoutrements of privilege. But here is an alternative account of the world these people are likely to see, from Amy Chua – herself an American from a racial minority:

> Poor and working-class whites have among the highest rates of unemployment and addiction [in the United States]. Life expectancy is declining for whites without a high school degree – something true of almost no other demographic, including high school dropouts from other racial groups. Education prospects for poor white children are extremely bleak. Private tutors and one-thousand-dollar SAT courses are completely cost prohibitive to poor or even working-class people – and poor whites don't benefit from affirmative action. Whereas most elite colleges do special outreach for racial minorities, they rarely send scouts to the backwoods of Kentucky. Out of roughly two hundred students in the Yale Law School class of 2019, there appears to be exactly one poor white – or three, if we include students from families living just above the federal poverty line. Administrators have described this class as the "most diverse" in the school's history.

Chua does not pretend American whites are the most persecuted people in America. "Whites may feel threatened, but they do not face mass, disproportionate incarceration," she writes later. "If many whites feel anxiety in today's America, many blacks feel an existential threat that seems never to end." But she's pointing to the blind spots that come to bear when a politics of identity obscures the experiences of class. To aggregate and compare, for example, the average earning capacity of white and non-white families, or to observe the dramatic overrepresentation of white men in politics, and to do so in isolation, is to reveal something important. But to lump everyone – white people included – into an undifferentiated identity category also obscures. Yes, whites are overrepresented. But, observes Chua, "working-class whites are decidedly not. Between 1999 and 2008, only 13 of the 783 members of Congress who served had spent more than a quarter of their adulthood in blue-collar jobs." Many working-class whites clearly felt alienated from the culture and institutions that surrounded them. Few people with any mainstream cultural or political power seemed to take that alienation seriously. It's easy to imagine that working-class whites felt themselves to be objects of contempt. And in an environment where such emotion can be commodified and turned into profit, someone like Donald Trump was always liable to come along. Whatever we might think of their alienation, these voters almost certainly considered themselves to be directing their contempt "upwards," which is why raging at "elites" was such a persistent touchstone of Trump's campaign. What followed illustrates what happens when people repay contempt with contempt.

This is something that some of the greatest advocates for racial justice have understood, including those so often cited in the course of contemptuous denunciation. Take James Baldwin. Among his most digitally disseminated quotes – the subject of a million tweets and memes – is that "We can disagree and still love each other unless your disagreement is rooted in my oppression and denial of my humanity and right to exist." Often, this is used as a way of signalling the end of exchange, the silence of contempt. But Baldwin's body of work stands as a monument to the refusal of contempt. It is shot through with sensitivity to its danger and warnings of its self-sabotage. In his 1968 novel *Tell Me How Long the Train's*

Been Gone, he explores this at length, showing that one of the many problems of giving oneself over to contempt *for* the other is that you thereby consent to the contempt *of* the other. Embracing contempt means agreeing on it as the moral currency of our social interactions – making it the coin of the realm. Moreover, by agreeing that contempt *can* be a licit means of judging a human being, we open the door to *self-contempt*, to seeing oneself through the eyes of the contemptuous other. Here he echoes W.E.B. Du Bois, who spoke of the moral effect of "the veil": that there are two worlds, locked away from one another by mutual contempt, such that, "despite much physical contact and daily intermingling, there is almost no continuity of intellectual life or point of transference where the thoughts and feelings of one race can come into direct contact and sympathy with thoughts and feelings of the other."

For Baldwin, the central moral challenge of *Tell Me How Long the Train's Been Gone* is how the protagonist (Leo Proudhammer) might save his brother, Caleb, and his lover, "Black Christopher," from the contempt that has taken over their own lives due to their own experiences of contempt and humiliation at the hands of white people, and especially the police. This is set up early in the novel. Ten-year-old Leo and seventeen-year-old Caleb are walking back to Harlem after an eventful Saturday night in the city. They know they will arrive home later than they had planned and, fearing certain reprisal at the hands of their father, the boys are rehearsing their alibi. An immigrant and an irascible drunk – who "brought with him from Barbados only black rum and a blacker pride" – their father embodies in Baldwin's novel the pathos of black nationalism. His every waking moment is filled with dreams of past glory: of African empires "greater and nobler than Rome or Judea, mightier than Egypt"; of "a race of kings, kings who had never been taken in battle, kings who had never been slaves." He thus has about him a certain air of nobility, and a corresponding disdain for his overlords in this new land – shopkeepers, pawnbrokers, welfare workers, landlords and, of course, police. And yet it is precisely their father's sense of superiority that renders him impotent. He is finally a pitiable character; even his frequent bouts of violence, most often directed at his own family, express a kind of pathetic, flailing rage. A rage, nonetheless, his sons do their best to avoid.

Nearing home, Leo and Caleb are still trying to get their story straight when they are stopped by two white policemen. There is no overt violence in the encounter. But what there is, is contempt – a contempt etched in the policemen's faces: "each mole, scar, pimple, nostril hair ... the eyes, the contemptuous eyes." It is a contempt communicated through the white hands that run over the bodies of the boys ("every touch humiliating, every touch obscene"). Unlike the boys' father, whose open disdain for Jews is a sign of his powerlessness, the contempt displayed by the policemen is the embodiment of the absolute power they have over the boys' bodies. That's what makes even the most seemingly innocuous touch obscene: it is the obscenity of unassailable, asymmetrical power. After the boys are sent on their way, Leo turns to his brother:

> "Caleb", I asked, "are white people, people?"
>
> "What are you talking about, Leo?"
>
> "I mean – are white people – *people*? People like us?"
>
> He looked down at me. His face was very strange and sad. It was a face I had never seen before. We climbed a few more stairs, very slowly. Then, "All I can tell you, Leo, is – well, *they* don't think they are."

Throughout his life, Baldwin insisted that the only way to overcome white ("Christian") contempt was not to give in to "pagan contempt" in kind; it was rather to discover both the particularity of and fraternity with other people. As he would write, for instance, to Angela Davis, "What the Americans do not realize is that a war between brothers, in the same cities, on the same soil, is not a racial war but a civil war." Or consider the way Leo Proudhammer himself loves, passionately, sexually, both Black Christopher and the white woman Barbara King – the former in defiance of white contempt for black militants; the later in defiance of black or "pagan" contempt for white women. Or, as Baldwin puts it elsewhere, "It is a terrible, an inexorable, law that one cannot deny the humanity of another without diminishing one's own: in the face of one's victim, one sees oneself." Hence Baldwin's extraordinary advice in *The Fire Next Time*:

> There is no reason for you to try to become like white people and there is no basis whatever for their impertinent assumption that *they* must accept *you*. The terrible thing, old buddy, is that *you* must accept *them*. And I mean that very seriously. You must accept them and accept them with love. For these innocent people have no other hope. They are, in effect, still trapped in a history which they do not understand; and until they understand it, they cannot be released from it. They have had to believe for many years, and for innumerable reasons, that black men are inferior to white men. Many of them, indeed, know better, but, as you will discover, people find it very difficult to act on what they know.

He does not pretend this approach is easy: "It demands great spiritual resilience not to hate the hater whose foot is on your neck, and an even greater miracle of perception and charity not to teach your child to hate." But this is nonetheless what he demands. Consider the language that shoots through his work: "a war between brothers"; "accept them with love"; "innocent people"; "many of them, indeed, know better." That is the moral centre of Baldwin's world, the irresistible force of his moral claims for racial justice: we are your brothers; you *know* this; and we call on your conscience for you to do right by your brother.

That is as far removed from a disposition of contempt as we can imagine. It imagines and addresses white people – even those who have believed "for many years, and for innumerable reasons, that black men are inferior to white men" – as moral agents. Not as irredeemable, privileged bigots to be excised from political community. It does not simply insult them, write them off and leave it at that in some solipsistic flourish of self-aggrandisement. You might say Baldwin's approach is positively Kantian. It is morally clear, insistent, strident, but at all times preserves an inalienable dignity of all as fully human interlocutors – albeit sometimes chronically misguided – with whom a common future is to be shared.

It is worth pointing out that Baldwin is not claiming that such an unwavering commitment to democratic fraternity and the dignity of others will guarantee justice, but rather that justice cannot be achieved without it. To put it simply, in a democracy, just ends cannot be pursued by unjust means – for, as Martin Luther King Jr insisted, "in the final analysis, means and ends must cohere because the end is pre-existent in the means, and ultimately destructive means cannot bring about constructive ends." Baldwin's approach of steadfastness and patience therefore turns the tables on those who would seek liberation through contempt – as with the Black Power movement of his day. Contempt is worse than unnecessary; it cannot succeed. It is *impotent*. For Baldwin, the problem isn't that Black Power is immoral on account of its militancy – indeed, he was not committed to nonviolence in the way that King was, and even felt an undeniable tenderness towards certain of its leaders (particularly Stokely Carmichael). It's more that Baldwin regarded the Black Power movement as a kind of tragic figure, like Leo Proudhammer's father, or Black Christopher. However much this figure bristles at the onslaught of daily humiliations and longs for the glories of a pre-colonial past, by committing itself to the kind of countervailing contempt that erupts into fraternal violence, Black Power condemns itself to all-consuming, self-destructive rage. Accordingly, Baldwin's convictions cannot be dismissed by appealing to political necessity. And certainly not now, given how implausible it is to argue that Baldwin was facing lesser injustices than those we face today.

Baldwin therefore poses a challenging question to those who see a democratic case for contempt: where is its track record of lasting change? Certainly, we can think of plenty of examples where contempt has underwritten decisive political action, but these examples always involve body-counts. It is the stuff of revolution and war – which is to say, the kind of action where enemies are eliminated or bent into submission.

That is fundamentally undemocratic, which is hardly surprising, because contempt refuses to imagine a political future in which one's opponents have a place.

Holding democracy in contempt

So what do we owe those with whom we might profoundly, even radically, disagree? In our time, the answer increasingly seems to be: *Nothing. Absolutely nothing*. We've come to regard our opponents as not much more than obstructions in the road, impediments standing between us and our desired end. They are there to be overcome, and whatever future we might envisage will be achieved either through their grudging acquiescence, or simply through their quiescence. We have therefore grown disinclined to consider what it might mean to go on together meaningfully as partners in a shared democratic project. To put it bluntly, we see no future with our political opponents because we feel we have nothing to learn from them.

This is reflected most starkly in the way we characterise one another: it's not that our opponents are partial, uninformed, mistaken, unwise, naive, that they are either overly cautious or needlessly impatient, or perhaps that they are simply animated by a different hierarchy of values that yields a moral intensity distinct from, but nonetheless commensurate with, our own. Instead, we tell ourselves, and anyone else who will listen, that our opponents are sub-rational, bigoted, toxic, dangerous, malignant, wilfully ignorant, cynically self-interested, fundamentally dishonest – in a word, inferior in every way that matters – and hence incapable of good-faith disagreement. They become reduced to tribal avatars: symbols to be appropriated for the prosecution of our politics. What matters, then, is not what these people actually say or do, but rather what we have decided they stand for, what their real agenda is. To borrow Agnes Callard's classification, we replace "literal speech" – where we "read [people's] words purely as vehicles for the contents of [their] beliefs" – with "messaging culture" – where we ignore the words and instead find the "evil intent or ulterior motive" behind them. As Callard explains:

> What makes speech truly free is the possibility of disagreement without enmity, and this is less a matter of what we can say, than how we can say it. "Cancel culture" is merely the logical extension of what we might call "messaging culture," in which every speech act is classified as friend or foe, in which literal content can barely be communicated, and in which very little faith exists as to the rational faculties of those being spoken to. In such a context, even the cry for "free speech" invites a nonliteral interpretation, as being nothing but the most efficient way for its advocates to acquire or consolidate power.

Once we take that approach towards our opponents, there is no longer any possibility of reasoning with them, because their stated reasons for why they believe what they believe cannot be taken at face value. And because rational debate is not possible, there is no point even taking part in the pretence of deliberation.

Is that how a democracy is meant to be? It would take a minimalist account of democracy to say so. And since we intend to argue that democracy cannot survive contempt, we must first acknowledge that minimalist accounts of democracy do exist, in which democracy connotes very little indeed: regular free and fair elections, the rule of law, tolerance of opposition political parties, and a set of rules that determine how publicly binding decisions get made. Other norms are implied in this, such as free speech, freedom of association, the availability of multiple sources of information, universal suffrage, and probably also some system of checks and balances.

A slightly more augmented version proceeds from the observation that society is not homogenous but is rather a collection of people with a diverse range of interests. It would be arbitrary to predetermine which of these interests is legitimate and should prevail, so democracy solves this through representation, in which each interest can find its reflection in government decisions. This model assumes a somewhat static vision of society, where people with fixed, already-formed interests gather to be represented. It requires nothing more of people than that. This is frequently called a "thin" conception of democracy.

But these "thin" versions of democracy cannot work in the abstract. People's interests cannot be represented without a citizenry educated enough to represent them; they cannot be balanced without in some way deliberating; they cannot deliberate without first respecting the right of the opposing side to be there as interlocutors, as equals. Indeed, these norms of respect and democratic equality are not an adjunct: they are the whole reason democracy exists, since, as Robert Talisse writes, "democracy is the proposition that a stable and decent society can be maintained in the absence of lords, masters, sovereigns, superiors, and kings. Democracy is the rejection of political hierarchy." That is to say, even thin democracy requires something to undergird it. Democracy requires a democratic culture. Without that, it becomes dysfunctional – destined to devolve into a mere ornament.

This insight yields the notion of "thick" democracy, which imagines society as a more dynamic organism where people can have their preferences and interests changed by their interactions with others. Democratic deliberation isn't merely a process of assertion and grudging compromise, but one of being mutually influenced. This is most fully exemplified in the soaring vision of Alexis de Tocqueville, who hoped the lived experience of cooperating together, despite political differences and partisan allegiances, as equal participants in a common effort, might cultivate the moral dispositions of sympathy, generosity, forbearance and mutual trust on which democratic life depend. For "feelings and ideas are renewed, the heart expands, and the human spirit develops only through the reciprocal action of human beings on one another." He does not describe this as a given, however. De Tocqueville is well aware that the very democratic desire to form associations, to find others of like mind, can readily be put to nefarious, anti-democratic ends by the skilled demagogue or the unprincipled press baron – by, say, purging the social body of political dissenters and racial minorities, or stoking the flames of populist resentment, or imposing an unassailable conformity by means of brute intimidation, or inciting a mob to lay waste to a chamber of representative government. Such dangers are ineradicable because nothing can guarantee the persistence and moral health of a democratic society other than the daily recommitment on the part of its members to go on together, to converse together, to learn from each other, to place themselves in one another's hands, to bear one another's burdens, to share one another's fate.

Democracy cannot therefore be merely antagonistic. Antagonism becomes democratic when it is orientated towards a common goal in which the antagonists are partners. Democratic hope is the expression of interdependence, a commitment to the discovery of a shared horizon of interests and aspirations. It stands in a tradition going back to Plato and Aristotle, which sees politics as not primarily about power (as it was for Machiavelli) or responsibility (for Max Weber) or even necessarily about order (for Hobbes), but rather as a kind of pastoral activity that emerges from a people's concern to care for the conditions of their common life – politics as "a cultivating, a tending, a taking care of beings and things," as Sheldon Wolin puts it. Democratic citizens are therefore bound together, and those bonds must be continually cultivated if they are to hold amid the strains of democratic deliberation. And that cultivation means nurturing practices which are themselves inseparable from the democratic aspiration: communal gathering, truthful speech, self-questioning, moral hesitation, silence, compromise, patience, frankness, forbearance, self-deprecating humour, play, and principled accommodation. As John Dewey recognised, it is precisely the "day by day adoption" of such practices and their "contagious diffusion in every phase of our common life" which enables democracy to become a moral reality. In short, democracy lives by and through such incidental acknowledgments of the moral reality of other persons. And as John Rawls argued, no democratic society, no matter the quality of its political institutions and traditions, can long withstand the corrosive effect of widespread envy, disdain, disgust, resentment, grudgingness, spitefulness and contemptuousness. Before long, Rawls feared, such sentiments will eat away at the affective bonds between citizens, to the point that it becomes impossible for them to see each other as equals.

This commitment – dare we call it Baldwinian – to a common life with a common future is the essence of democracy. Democracy's great virtue is that it offers a perpetually deliberative politics. It undulates with the regular changing of governments, the relatively short-term and conditional nature of both victory and defeat. It therefore allows us to avoid a "winner-takes-all" approach to politics in which a future with those on the other side of political debate need not be imagined. We might surmise, then, that the more "winner-takes-all" our politics grows, the less healthily democratic it becomes. And we can expect that, over time, each side keeps raising the stakes of disagreement to the point that any concession to the other is akin to a perfidious betrayal – a kind of appeasement when what is required is total resistance.

This is exactly what we're seeing in America. As Jonathan Haidt observes in an essay recently published in *The Atlantic*:

> the enhanced virality of social media … made it more hazardous to be seen fraternizing with the enemy or even failing to attack the enemy with sufficient vigor. On the right, the term RINO (Republican in Name Only) was superseded in 2015 by the more contemptuous term *cuckservative*, popularized on Twitter by Trump supporters. On the left, social media launched callout culture in the years after 2012, with transformative effects on university life and later on politics and culture throughout the English-speaking world.

The logic of contempt is therefore not merely hatred of the other side, but the search for enemies within, for once contempt is routine, there is no reason to stop at mere party-political differences. The result, argues Haidt, is a deeply undemocratic stifling of dissent that plays out differently across the political spectrum. On the right, the traditional conservatism that might care for the integrity of the electoral system or the enduring institutions of government is cowed by a loud conspiratorial narrative of stolen elections and the "deep state." On the left, liberal progressives who believe injustices can be, and are being, shed, are cowed by a critical postmodern narrative that holds almost every prevailing social structure – including even notions of free speech – to be a structure of power and oppression. Hence the rapid transition of a statement such as "I don't see race" from being a salutary progressive epithet to evidence of an eye roll–inducing racism.

The right regards its dissenters as traitors and charges them with treason, for which the traditional punishment is death – "hence," says Haidt, "Hang Mike Pence." The left opts for charges of -isms and -phobias that constitute hatred and harm for a marginalised group. The punishment for that is public shaming. What's notable for our purposes is that both are expressions of contempt; not of disagreement, but of being irredeemably beyond the pale. This is a remarkable sleight of hand, where contempt is founded on constantly changing, and highly contested, moral ground. These are not cases where people contemn others for falling short of a widely agreed moral standard. It is not the contempt for a thief, paedophile or murderer. It is not even Camille's contempt for Paul in *Le Mépris*, in which both agree that bartering a spouse's sexual favours for one's own career advancement is an immoral thing to do, however much Paul denies the allegation. Contemporary political contempt forms before moral consensus is achieved and tries to set new norms through intimidation. It believes that if only we call enough people "cuckservatives" or "racists" loudly and publicly – if we repeat that our opponents are "selling out the country" or are "on the wrong side of history" – we can redefine society's moral parameters by brute force. This is moralism without any of the hard work of moral persuasion. The result is that even in the university, an institution built on freedom of thought and truth-seeking, we see students reporting that they censor their views because they are afraid to speak their minds. We should be unsurprised that we see evidence of people being cowed into silence, but little evidence of consensus.

Over the last decade, we've watched this dynamic play itself out repeatedly within and between opposing sides around such matters as sexual harassment and abuse, racial injustice, police brutality, climate change, membership of the European Union, vaccine hesitancy, LGBTIQ discrimination, religious freedom, and abortion. On each count, worthy goals of mutual consideration and common pursuit have been either brought undone or had their broader appeal severely compromised by the "hashtag politics" of moral intransigence (#GetBrexitDone, #BlackLivesMatter, #DefundthePolice, #SilenceIsViolence, #StayWoke, #ThereIsNoPlanetB, #IGotVaccinated, #SaveRoe, et cetera). Declaration and posturing take the place of persuasion, claims of moral superiority undermine the hard work of gradual consensus-building, and the vigilante impulse for summary judgment rules out the possibility of complexity, ambiguity, degrees of complicity, or doubt.

As we've seen, there is an undeniable pleasure that accompanies this kind of moral clarity. We prize it in ourselves, and we demand it from the politicians, pundits and opinion-makers we follow. But the problem with "moral clarity," as George Packer writes, "is how much of life and news gets lost in its glare. It overpowers subjects more than it illuminates them. Writers stop seeing the little flaws and contradictions of actual life, and stop wanting to – they and their readers have only to bask in the warmth of a blinding glow." Consider, alternatively, philosopher Adam Piovarchy's perceptive assessment of how this plays out in the politics of vaccination:

> One of the best things we can do is make getting vaccinated seem normal, as simply part of a collective project, rather than yet another marker of tribal identity in a culture war. It's much harder to frame being unvaccinated as a marker of independence, free-thought or suspicion of the government if no one is arguing with you. Instead of pushing harder, lower their resistance.

Whatever short-term gratification this culture of implacable stances may provide, however enjoyable the hot-takes and take-downs, it is catastrophic for our democratic culture. At the heart of what might be called the moral distinctiveness of democratic politics is an acute awareness of the inevitability of disagreement within the common life of a people whom, in Michael Oakeshott's phrase, "chance or choice have brought together." It governs people whose connections are strictly contingent and who cannot therefore appeal to any extrinsic principle or quasi-divine adjudicator to settle matters of contention once and for all.

The greatest danger to the stability of democratic life is therefore not when disagreements become interminable, but when they become *incommensurable* – which is to say, when both parties get caught in a state of mutual incomprehension. That certainly seems to be the case in the United States. Only about 2 per cent each of Trump and Biden voters think those who voted for the other candidate understand them "very well," according to Pew research, and the other 98 per cent are probably correct. The United States is becoming a nation of aliens, unknown and unknowable to each other, with no common narrative to bind them. Probably the most commonly heard lament of progressives after the election of Donald Trump was that they woke up overnight to a country they no longer recognised. Four years earlier, those cheering for Mitt Romney were found by researchers to be twice as sad in the wake of Barack Obama's victory than Bostonians were after the Boston Marathon bombings. Such a depth of incommensurability is new, as Chua observes: "at different times in the past, both the American Left and the American Right have stood for group-transcending values. Neither does today."

This, in essence, was the fault that the late Justice Ruth Bader Ginsburg found with the US Supreme Court's 1973 decision of *Roe v. Wade*, which has turned so recently pyrotechnic. Her criticisms were several, including that it was decided on a questionable legal basis that left it vulnerable to challenge. But more relevantly for our purposes, she believed the court's ruling effectively arrested the momentum that had been slowly building in state legislatures and district courts towards the decriminalisation of abortion:

> The political process was moving in the early 1970s, not swiftly enough for advocates of quick, complete change, but majoritarian institutions were listening and acting. Heavy-handed judicial intervention was difficult to justify and appears to have provoked, not resolved, conflict.

Her point is that by "settling" the matter too early and with too much brute force, the court created the circumstances in which the arguments on either side could harden into a culture war: irreconcilable claims of absolute value (pro-Life *versus* pro-Choice), rendering each side morally unintelligible to the other. History has proven her correct, and the politics of abortion has been tearing American democracy apart ever since.

For many, the prospect of what we might think of as this kind of democratic divorce is not just tolerable – it is eagerly anticipated. Along any number of our current political faultlines, each side has become convinced that their lives, and the life of the nation as a whole, would be a good deal better off if their opponents just went away. We have earlier noted the "Quexit" meme after the 2019 Australian federal election, and we saw a similar line of thought among American progressives who spruiked the benefits of certain states seceding from the union should Donald Trump be re-elected in 2020. Such incommensurability is what happens when "thin" democracy is all you have. Contempt thins out democracy until finally it reaches the point of dysfunction. America provides the signal case of this, probably because it is the environment most dominated by the media/social-media contempt machine we have earlier described. The result is a country that now barely has an agreed set of facts over which its citizens can deliberate; a place with democratic trappings, but few of the underlying preconditions of a democratic culture. That is what a thin democracy looks like. It would be more accurate to describe it as a post-democracy.

How, then, might we describe the bond that *must* exist between democratic citizens for democracy to flourish? Simone Weil was incredibly perceptive to draw the analogy between political institutions and what she calls the "symbolic language" that exists between lovers: the exchange of rings, letters or other tokens of mutual devotion. These symbols neither initiate the relationship nor ensure its stability, any more than the beauty of the wedding ceremony or the value of the rings guarantees the inner health of the marriage. But the symbols are not hollow, either. Rather, they cultivate the conditions of the relationship so that it acquires depth, complexity, longevity and fecundity; so that it grows, as Weil puts it, "like a plant."

At this point, Weil inherits the tradition of John Milton, Hegel, John Stuart Mill, and taken up in our time by philosophers such as Axel Honneth and Stanley Cavell. These thinkers picture politics as analogous to a marriage – a particular type of relationship in which two persons, who are bound together by nothing more substantial than a reciprocal devotion, discover through their life together the "ethical conditions" that allow their union to persist. Marriage, then, has its formal arrangements – like democracy – but cannot be reduced to them. Its health requires something thicker than a mere legal agreement. It is a bond that must be cultivated, lest it thin out to the point it finally breaks.

It seems fitting that we should arrive at this metaphor, given our discussion of contempt began with Michelle Mason's account of Camille and Paul's marriage in *Le Mépris*. The example comes from cinema, but the central insight – that marriage cannot survive contempt – is not merely a trope of popular culture. In 1992, John Gottman and Robert Levenson developed a model of marital failure, based on how couples speak to one another, that continues to form the basis of relationship research. They identified four key predictors of divorce – what Gottman later called the "Four Horsemen of the Apocalypse" – which cascade until they overwhelm the relationship. These "Horsemen" are criticism, defensiveness, contempt and stonewalling.

Among these, contempt was the strongest predictor, the single most important sign, that the marriage is in trouble. And it is here that we run into the one terrifying difference between democracy and marriage. Married couples at least have the final option of divorce. Democracies do not. Their equivalent is a civil war. It is not for nothing that serious American thinkers are debating whether the United States is presently heading for another one.

A common technique used by relationship counsellors requires each member of a couple to answer a series of questions as though they were the other. In this way, each person is forced to articulate the other's grievances and feelings, with the other person listening. It reveals the extent to which each understands the other's perspective, but it also demands that each listens seriously enough to the other to be able to speak accurately for them. In a word, it demands attentiveness. This returns us to Simone Weil, who offers a distinctive use of attentiveness – and the related term, attention – in political life.

Attention is what is owed to the moral reality of other people. It is the refusal to reduce them to a caricature, a stereotype, a mere generality that can be summarised and summarily dismissed. Transposed into the concrete practice of public debate, this requires at the very least that we engage with the best version of our opponents' arguments, rather than be content with the sneering demolition of caricatures. And it demands that media outlets shelve their partisan preferences enough to present these arguments as faithfully as possible. We must imagine ourselves on the counsellor's couch, being asked to give the most just account of the other's view, such that it resonates not with our image of them, but with their image of themselves. Now imagine what our public conversation would look like if that was our habit.

As information becomes ever more curated and siloed, as we retreat into Google's "filter bubbles" or hand over our editorial gatekeeping to Silicon Valley algorithms, this is becoming increasingly difficult. How often do news events first reach us packaged in commentary, whether as an op-ed or a pithy remark in a retweet? How often do we encounter a contrary view only by seeing it scathingly criticised at the hands of one of our own team? How often do those criticisms attribute unknowable, cynical motives to our opponents with an extraordinary level of confidence? To overcome this, and to see one another clearly and rightly, requires a deliberate effort. It requires patience and time. But it is through this unhurried act of seeing that we can discover the form of words that best describes the other.

The act of attention does not gloss over the flaws and faults and weaknesses and petty prejudices of another person, but neither does it take those faults and prejudices as proof that the other person is a moral inferior, unworthy of further conversation. Attention resists both crassness and condescension. Truly attending to another, and opening ourselves up to the possibility of reciprocal learning, requires nothing less than relinquishing the inclination to use another person as a means to our own end, whether that be our own self-aggrandisement, or even as raw material for the production of our own political rhetoric. It demands a willingness to have our political goals redefined for the sake of shared understanding and in the hope of mutual transformation. That is the purpose of a moral community, like a marriage or a democracy.

Contempt, on the other hand, is for Weil "the contrary of attention." It corrodes the conditions of political community by disallowing the possibility of moral encounter. Where contempt inflates the self, attentiveness insists we try to grasp what the world looks like through the other's eyes. Where contempt generalises and totalises, attentiveness reckons with the ethical particularity of the other. Where contempt flattens people into objects, attentiveness sees them in their depth. And, perhaps most tellingly, where contempt rushes to judgment – especially in our hypersonic digital culture – attentiveness demands what Weil calls an "interval of hesitation." And note how corrosive things become when we eliminate such intervals, even tiny ones, such as when Twitter unleashed its Retweet button. The previously required act of copying and pasting forced people to read what they wanted to share and think about whether they wanted to go to the trouble of sharing it. The Retweet button instantly transformed this act into something impulsive and performative. Now, at least 60 per cent of the news stories shared on social media have not been read by the person sharing them.

Far too many of us have become unpractised in the habits of patience, reciprocity and free exchange, which are the lifeblood of any healthy democratic culture. Particularly under the conditions of the pandemic, during which we grew ever more terrified of our fellow breathers, unable to share the same air or occupy the same space, and taking solace instead in online "connection," we have become profoundly unreal to one another and therefore inattentive to the moral reality of our fellow citizens. This is perhaps the greatest irony: for all of the talk of the "attention economy," attention is precisely what our social-media-saturated age disallows. We are living in a time of contempt. And the future of our democratic life depends on whether we can resist it.

SOURCES

1 "We may live in the first period": Mark Manson, "Living in the age of outrage," markmanson.net/outrage, 26 May 2017.

2 repeated surveys reveal: Betsy Cooper, Daniel Cox, E.J. Dionne Jr, Rachel Lienesch, Robert P. Jones and William A. Galston, *How Immigration and Concerns about Cultural Change Are Shaping the 2016 Election*, Public Religion Research Institute/Brookings, 23 June 2016. See also Michael I. Norton and Samuel R. Sommers, "Whites see racism as a zero-sum game that they are now losing," *Perspectives on Psychological Science*, vol. 6, no. 3, 2011, pp. 215–18; Don Goneya, "Majority of white Americans say they believe whites face discrimination," NPR, 24 October 2017.

2 The English-language internet: See, for example, Belinda Luscombe, "Fighting with a family member over politics? Try these four steps," *Time*, 19 February 2021; Beverley B. Palmer, "Four science-based strategies to tame angry political debate and encourage tolerance," *The Conversation*, 28 February 2020; Elizabeth Bernstein, "Loathe your loved one's politics? Here's some advice," *The Wall Street Journal*, 19 October 2020.

2 frequently terminating friendships: Tovia Smith, "'Dude, I'm done: when politics tears families and friendships apart," *All Things Considered*, NPR, 27 October 2020.

2 In 2016, the Pew Research Center: Pew Research Center, *Partnership and Political Animosity in 2016*, 22 June 2016.

2 By 2020, Pew found: Amina Dunn, "Few Trump or Biden supporters have close friends who back the opposing candidate," Pew Research Center, 18 September 2020.

2 "It's absolutely staggering": Shannon Molloy, "Australia has never been more divided on social and political issues: are we becoming the US?", News.com.au, 12 October 2018.

2 Surveys show that voters: Ian McCallister and Sarah M. Cameron, *Trends in Australian Political Opinion*, Australian National University, Canberra, 2016.

2–3 ideologically they have scarcely moved: "Australian Election 2016" and "Australian Election 2017," PoliticalCompass.org.

3 the 2013 Australian Election Study: Luke Mansillo and Nick Evershed, "Australian politics becoming more polarised," *The Guardian*, 7 August 2014.

3 Public broadcaster SBS: Glen Fuller, "How to survive your conservative relatives this Christmas," *SBS News*, 23 December 2013.

3 But it was taken seriously: Anne Tiernan, Jacob Deem and Jennifer Menzies, "Queensland to all those #Quexiteers: don't judge, try to understand us,"

The Conversation, 22 May 2019. See also Rebecca Varcoe, "Why blaming Queensland won't fix Australia," *Junkee*, 20 May 2019.

4 Clinton later conceded: Hillary Rodham Clinton, *What Happened?*, Simon & Schuster, New York, 2017, p. 418.

4 "I saw more undecided voters shift": Diane Hessan, "Understanding the undecided voters," *Boston Globe*, 21 November 2016.

5 "Just when Hillary Clinton said": Katie Reilly, "Read Hillary Clinton's 'basket of deplorables' remarks about Donald Trump supporters," *Time*, 10 September 2016.

5 "It would have been different if": Roxanne Roberts, "Hillary Clinton's 'deplorables' speech shocked voters five years ago – but some feel it was prescient," *The Washington Post*, 31 August 2021.

5 "Boy, that second word is tough": Eli Stokols and Louis Nelson, "Trump channels 'Les Deplorables,' says Hillary Clinton's secret service detail should disarm," *Politico*, 16 September 2016.

5 A 2020 survey found: "Dueling realities: amid multiple crises, Trump and Biden supporters see different priorities and futures for the nation," Public Religion Research Institute, 19 October 2020.

6 "We feel invisible": Zach Hope, "'Weak-kneed and jelly-bellied": Nats' life at the Queensland coalface is getting complicated," *The Age*, 20 October 2021.

8 Moreover, Australian social-media users: Alexander Bor and Michael Bang Petersen, "The psychology of online political hostility: a comprehensive, cross-national test of the mismatch hypothesis," *American Political Science Review*, vol. 116, no. 1, 2022, pp. 1–18.

8 Australians' main news source: Roy Morgan, "It's official: internet is Australia's main source of news; TV remains most trusted," 21 August 2020.

8–9 Nearly a quarter of Australians: Sora Park, Caroline Fisher, Kieran McGuinness, Jee Young Lee and Kerry McCallum, *Digital News Report: Australia 2021*, University of Canberra, 2021.

9 "elite media": Michael Koziol, "Making Australia great again: the Trump effect takes hold," *The Sydney Morning Herald*, 18 November 2016.

11 Michelle Mason: Michelle Mason, "Contempt as a moral attitude," *Ethics*, vol. 113, no. 2, 2003, pp. 234–72.

12 "badbeing": Macalester Bell, *Hard Feelings: The Moral Psychology of Contempt*, Oxford University Press, Oxford, 2013, p. 39.

12 In Mason's formulation: Mason, p. 247.

13 Such action is necessary: Mason, p. 241.

13 it is *performative*: Bell, p. 46.

15 "Asking people what they want": Megan Davis, Cheryl Saunders, Mark McKenna, Shireen Morris, Christopher Mayes and Maria Giannacopoulos, "The Uluru

Statement from Heart, one year on: can a First Nations voice yet be heard?", *ABC Religion and Ethics*, 26 May 2018.

15–16 Frederick Douglass's reflections: Frederick Douglass, *My Bondage and My Freedom*, Dover Publications, Mineola, 1969, p. 100.

16 "downward contempt": William Ian Miller, "Upward contempt," *Political Theory*, vol. 23, no. 2, 1995, pp. 476–99.

17 as Jon Ronson has shown: Jon Ronson, *So You've Been Publicly Shamed*, Pan Macmillan, Sydney, 2015.

18 outlets led by *The Australian*: See, for example, Caroline Overington, "Taxpayers billed for *Q&A* activist Yassmin Abdel-Magied's grand tour of Islamic regimes," *The Australian*, 15 February 2017.

19 "risks losing the capacity to forgive": Mason, p. 249.

19 "a deep dismissal": Thomas E. Hill Jr, *Respect, Pluralism, and Justice: Kantian Perspectives*, Oxford University Press, New York, 2000, p. 60.

21 "At times one cannot": Immanuel Kant, *The Metaphysics of Morals*, in *Practical Philosophy*, trans. and ed. Mary J. Gregor, Cambridge University Press, Cambridge, 1996, pp. 579–80.

21 "enjoying and hating finely": Aristotle, *Aristotle: Selections*, trans. Terence Irwin and Gail Fine, Hackett Publishing Company, Cambridge, 1995, p. 445.

21 "the censure of vice": Kant, p. 580.

21 "looking down on people": David Sussman, "Above and beneath contempt," in *The Moral Psychology of Contempt*, ed. Michelle Mason, Rowman and Littlefield, London, 2019, p. 153. For some examples of this work, see William Ian Miller, *The Anatomy of Disgust*, Harvard University Press, Cambridge, 1997; Kate Abramson, "A sentimentalist's defense of contempt, shame, and disdain," in *The Oxford Handbook of Philosophy of Emotion*, ed. Peter Goldie, Oxford University Press, New York, 2009.

22 "recognition respect": Stephen L. Darwall, "The two kinds of respect," in *Ethics and Personality: Essays in Moral Psychology*, ed. John Deigh, University of Chicago Press, 1992, pp. 65–78.

23 Broadly, Bell says: Bell, pp. 148–9. Emphasis removed from the original.

24 recourse to literature: Bell, p. 158.

24 "appreciate the reasons": Bell, p. 225.

24 "inner moral state": Jean Hampton, "The retributive idea," in Jeffrie G. Murphy and Jean Hampton, *Forgiveness and Mercy*, Cambridge University Press, Cambridge, 1988, p. 152.

26 "whether such contempt": Mason, p. 269.

26 William Miller insists: Miller, "Upward Contempt", p. 496.

26 "Every person is now entitled": Miller, *The Anatomy of Disgust*, p. 234.

27 "Not long ago": Amy Chua, *Political Tribes: Group Instinct and the Fate of Nations*, Bloomsbury, New York, 2018, p. 10.

27 "deformation and excess": Mason, p. 248.

27 one American study has shown: Steven Hawkins, Daniel Yudkin, Miriam Juan-Torres and Tim Dixon, *Hidden Tribes: A Study of America's Polarized Landscape*, More in Common, New York, 2018.

29 "Air is the medium": Luce Irigaray, *The Way of Love*, trans. H. Bostic and S. Pluháček, Continuum, London, 2002, p. 67.

29 "quintessence of the human condition": Hannah Arendt, *The Human Condition*, University of Chicago Press, Chicago, 1958, p. 2.

30 "We do not breathe well": Ralph Waldo Emerson, "Address to the citizens of Concord on the fugitive slave law (1851)," in *The Selected Lectures of Ralph Waldo Emerson*, ed. Ronald A Bosco and Joel Myerson, University of Georgia Press, London, 2005, pp. 169–85.

30 "environmental threat to social peace": Jeremy Waldron, *The Harm in Hate Speech*, Harvard University Press, Cambridge, 2012, p. 4.

30 "*Whatever* matters to human beings": Sissela Bok, *Lying: Moral Choice in Public and Private Life*, Vintage Books, New York, p. 31.

32 beleaguered *New York Times*: See Susan E. Tifft and Alex S. Jones, *The Trust: The Private and Powerful Family Behind the New York Times*, Little, Brown and Company, New York, 1999, pp. 41–46.

32 none of his editorial scruples: Paul Starr, *The Creation of the Media: Political Origins of Modern Communication*, Basic Books, New York, 2004, p. 256.

32 "sewers and morgue fields": Tifft and Jones, p. 46. For a vivid illustration, see Paul Collins, *The Murder of the Century: The Gilded Age Crime That Scandalized a City and Sparked the Tabloid Wars*, Broadway Books, New York, 2011.

32 So the tabloids adopted a tone: Michael Schudson, *Discovering the News: A Social History of American Newspapers*, Basic Books, New York, 1978, pp. 97–106; Starr, pp. 257–59.

33 "The majority of the public": William A. Swanberg, *Citizen Hearst: A Biography of William Randolph Hearst*, Charles Scribner's Sons, New York, 1961, p. 138.

34 The newspapers had their war: See Christopher B. Daly, *Covering America: A Narrative History of a Nation's Journalism*, University of Massachusetts Press, Amherst, 2018, pp. 132–38; Jill Lepore, *These Truths: A History of the United States*, W.W. Norton and Company, New York, 2018, pp. 336–37.

34 "the public is even more fond": Schudson, p. 99.

34 "circulation means advertising": Starr, p. 257.

34 Both men inherited the logic: Schudson, pp. 14–31.

36 Technologist Andy Baio: Andy Baio, "72 hours of #Gamergate," *The Message*, 28 October 2014.

36 a New York University study: Steve Rajthe, Jay J. van Bavel and Sander van der Linden, "Out-group animosity drives engagement on social media," *Proceedings of the National Academy of Sciences*, vol. 118, no. 26, 2021, p. 2.

36 "moral emotion is the key": William J. Brady, Julian A. Wills, John T. Jost, Joshua A. Tucker and Jay J. Van Bavel, "Emotion shapes the diffusion of moralized content in social networks," *Proceedings of the National Academy of Sciences*, vol. 114, no. 28, 2017, pp. 7313–18.

36 "status-driven individuals": Bor and Petersen, pp. 1–18.

37 in the milder language of one of these studies: Rajthe, van Balen and van der Linden, p. 7.

37 Rosenstein told *The Guardian*: Paul Lewis, "'Our minds can be hijacked': the tech insiders who fear a smartphone dystopia," *The Guardian*, 6 October 2017.

37 "We might have just handed": Alex Kantrowitz, "The man who built the retweet: 'We handed a loaded weapon to 4-year-olds,'" *Buzzfeed News*, 24 July 2019.

38 "The thing I saw at Facebook": *60 Minutes*, CBS, 3 October 2021.

38 an analysis in *Science*: Soroush Vosoughi, Deb Roy and Sinan Aral, "The spread of true and false news online," *Science*, vol. 359, 2018, pp. 1146–51.

38–39 "the Internet shows signs of creating": Bernard Williams, *Truth and Truthfulness: An Essay in Genealogy*, Princeton University Press, Princeton, 2010, p. 216.

39 "outrage factory": Michael P. Lynch, *Know-It-All Society: Truth and Arrogance in Political Culture*, Liveright, New York, 2020, p. 44.

39 "an anger machine": Siva Vaidhyanathan, *Antisocial Media: How Facebook Disconnects Us and Undermines Democracy*, Oxford University Press, New York, 2018, p. 51.

40 Alexis de Tocqueville's sense: Alexis de Tocqueville, *Democracy in America*, trans. Arthur Goldhammer, Library of America, New York, 2004, pp. 600–1.

40 It is no wonder: Tifft and Jones, *The Trust*, 45–46.

40–41 Lord John Reith acknowledged: John C.W. Reith, *Broadcast over Britain*, Hodder and Stoughton, 1924, pp. 33–34; see also K.S. Inglis, *This Is the ABC: The Australian Broadcasting Commission, 1932–1983*, Melbourne University Press, Carlton, 1983, p. 12.

42 "going viral is a goal": Emily Bell, "The 2015 Hugh Cudlipp Lecture," *The Guardian*, 28 January 2015.

42 The relentless logic of this new environment: George Packer, *Last Best Hope: America in Crisis and Renewal*, Jonathan Cape, London, 2021, pp. 204–5.

43 "tabloid model": Daniel C. Hallin and Paolo Mancini (eds), *Comparing Media Systems: Three Models of Media and Politics*, Cambridge University Press, Cambridge, 2004.

43 "the tabloidisation of everything": Bell.

43 "To survive, media companies": Franklin Foer, *World without Mind: The Existential Threat of Big Tech*, Penguin, New York, 2017, p. 7.

45 "One of the things we know": German Lopez, "Research says there are ways to reduce social bias. Calling people racist isn't one of them," *Vox*, 30 July 2018.

45 As one such voter told *The Atlantic*: Chris Bodenner, "If you want identity politics, identity politics is what you'll get," *The Atlantic*, 11 November 2016.

46 "Poor and working-class whites": Chua, pp. 171–75.

48 Here he echoes W.E.B. Du Bois: W.E.B. Du Bois, "The souls of black folk," in *Writings*, ed. Nathan Huggins, Library of America, New York, 1986, pp. 488–89.

49 "each mole, scar, pimple": James Baldwin, *Tell Me How Long the Train's Been Gone*, in *Later Novels*, Library of America, New York, p. 47.

49 As he would write, for instance: James Baldwin, "An open letter to my sister Angela Y. Davis," in *The Cross of Redemption: Uncollected Writings*, ed. Randall Kenan, Vintage, New York, 2010, p. 259.

50 "it is a terrible, an inexorable, law": James Baldwin, "Fifth Avenue, Uptown: A letter from Harlem," in *Collected Essays*, ed. Toni Morrison, Library of America, New York, 1998, p. 179.

50 "There is no reason for you to try": James Baldwin, *The Fire Next Time*, in *Collected Essays*, ed. Toni Morrison, Library of America, New York, 1998, pp. 293–94.

51 "means and ends must cohere": Martin Luther King Jr, "A Christmas sermon on peace," in *A Testament of Hope: Essential Writings and Speeches of Martin Luther King, Jr*, ed. James Melvin Washington, HarperCollins, San Francisco, 1986, p. 257.

53 "What makes speech truly free": Agnes Callard, "Should we cancel Aristotle?", *The New York Times*, 21 July 2020.

54 as Robert Talisse writes: Robert B. Talisse, *Sustaining Democracy: What We Owe to the Other Side*, Oxford University Press, New York, 2021, p. 24.

54 "feelings and ideas are renewed": De Tocqueville, p. 601.

55 "a cultivating, a tending": Sheldon Wolin, "Hannah Arendt: democracy and the political," in *Fugitive Democracy and Other Essays*, ed. Nicholas Xenos, Princeton University Press, Princeton, 2016, p. 248.

55 "day by day adoption": John Dewey, "Democratic ends need democratic methods for their realization," in *The Later Words of John Dewey, 1925–1953*, vol. 4, ed. Jo Ann Boydston, Southern Illinois University Press, Carbondale, 1988, p. 368.

55–56 as John Rawls argued: John Rawls, *A Theory of Justice*, Belknap Press, Cambridge, 1971, pp. 470–1, 530–41.

56 As Jonathan Haidt observes: Jonathan Haidt, "Why the past ten years of American life have been so uniquely stupid," *The Atlantic*, 11 April 2022.

57 students reporting that they censor their views: Emma Camp, "I came to college eager to debate. I found self-censorship," *The New York Times*, 8 March 2022.

58 the problem with "moral clarity": George Packer, *Last Best Hope: America in Crisis and Renewal*, Jonathan Cape, London, 2021, p. 207.

58 "One of the best things we can do": Adam Piovarchy, "Moral superiority is no way to encourage people to be vaccinated," *ABC Religion and Ethics*, 11 November 2021.

59 "chance or choice have brought together": Michael Oakeshott, "Political education," in *Rationalism in Politics and Other Essays*, Liberty Fund, Indianapolis, 1991, p. 44.

59 according to Pew research: Amina Dunn, Jocelyn Kelly, Alissa Scheller, Chris Baronavski and Carrol Doherty, "Voters say those on the other side 'don't get' them. Here's what they want them to know," Pew Research Center, 17 December 2020.

59 were found by researchers: Lamar Pierce, Todd Rogers and Jason Snyder, "Losing hurts: the happiness impact of partisan electoral loss," Harvard Kennedy School, 5 March 2015.

59 "at different times": Chua, p. 178.

60 "The political process was moving": Ruth B. Ginsburg, "Some thoughts on autonomy and equality in relation to *Roe v Wade*," *North Carolina Law Review*, vol. 63, no. 2, 1985, pp. 375–86.

60 we saw a similar line of thought: David French explored this phenomenon in his book *Divided We Fall: America's Secession Threat and How to Restore Our Nation*, St Martin's Press, New York, 2020.

61 "like a plant": Simone Weil, "The legitimacy of the provisional government," trans. Peter Winch, *Philosophical Investigations*, vol. 10, no. 2, 1987, p. 88.

61 In 1992, John Gottman and Robert Levenson: John M. Gottman and Robert W. Levenson, "Marital processes predictive of later dissolution: behavior, physiology, and health," *Journal of Personality and Social Psychology*, vol. 63, no. 2, 1992, pp. 221–33.

61 "Four Horsemen of the Apocalypse": John Gottman, "A theory of marital dissolution and stability," *Journal of Family Psychology*, vol. 7, no. 1, 1993, pp. 57–75.

63 "the contrary of attention": Simone Weil, "Forms of the implicit love of god," in *Waiting for God*, trans. Emma Craufurd, Harper & Row, New York, 1951, p. 95.

63 "interval of hesitation": Simone Weil, "The Iliad, or the Poem of Force," in *An Anthology*, ed. Siân Miles, Penguin, London, 2005, p. 194.

64 Now, at least 60 per cent of the news: Lynch, p. 41.

Correspondence

Malcolm Turnbull

For many years Hugh White has argued that Australia should not assume the continued presence of superior American power in our region, but rather accommodate ourselves to the reality that China will become the hegemon in this hemisphere as the United States is in its own.

Whether you agree with White or not, these regular doses of realpolitik are invigorating but in this latest Quarterly Essay, White has strayed into sweeping generalisations and, frankly, "alternative facts" to embellish his argument. I was disappointed that a scholar of his standing would do so.

White's description of Australian foreign policy is simply wrong – in his view we have been passive clients of the United States, always looking to our great and powerful friend in Washington to solve all our China problems. Thus he suggests decisions taken by my government to enact laws on foreign interference and the 5G network were inspired by the Trump administration. He adds that by 2017, "Turnbull had repositioned Australia as the most stridently anti-Chinese country in the region, and indeed globally." He then goes on to say that in August 2018, I "tried to back-pedal with a major 'reset' speech at the University of New South Wales."

Nowhere in this description does White consider whether the extent of foreign (mostly Chinese) espionage and other influence in Australia warranted new legislation, any more than he considers whether the ban on Huawei and ZTE from the 5G network was justified on security grounds. The reader is left to assume that White believes it would have been more prudent for Australia not to bother about these security threats.

The truth is that both the foreign interference legislation and 5G decisions were carefully considered, calibrated responses to real threats. Great care was taken, especially with the 5G decision, not to arouse unnecessary resentment, and our announcement was deliberately very low-key. We went to great lengths, without success, to find a way to mitigate the risks so that we would not have to ban Huawei. The decisions were taken by the Australian government in Australia's national interest and were not dictated or encouraged by any other government, including that of the United States. Indeed, as I have described in my memoir, *A Bigger Picture*, we were ahead of the United States in our assessment of the risks posed by the very different architecture of 5G wireless technologies.

As for the "back-pedal" – the background to that was quite the reverse of White's description. The foreign interference and influence legislation was introduced at the end of 2017. The Labor Opposition had not agreed to support its passage through the Senate and there was considerable pressure from China to encourage the government to drop it and for Labor not to support it.

Once Labor had agreed to support the legislation and it was passed, we needed to create an opportunity for China to elegantly discontinue its pressure campaign. So I gave a speech at the UNSW in August 2018 which did not take a backward step on any matter of policy, but was warm in its tone and context, pointing to the considerable achievements from Sino–Australian cooperation in science and research. This was designed as an opportunity for China to reset and was not a "back-pedal" in any respect.

While China's strategy of becoming the dominant power in our hemisphere is unchanging, its tactics are thoroughly flexible and when one line of pressure or coercion fails to achieve its objective, China will switch to another approach but generally needs the appearance of a catalyst to provide the exit ramp. The recent change of government is a good example of this.

Where White is on firmer ground is in his criticism of the gratuitously belligerent bluster about China from Scott Morrison and, especially, Peter Dutton. The absurdity of some of Dutton's comments about Taiwan was underlined for me in November 2021 at the Halifax Security Conference, when one American four-star after another wryly observed, "Your defence minister is more forward-leaning on Taiwan than our president."

And White is correct in saying that this belligerent rhetoric was designed to pander to a political and media constituency in Australia, undermining Australian security and prosperity in return for some favourable headlines in the Murdoch media.

White makes the mistake of swallowing whole the rhetoric around AUKUS. He describes it as "a major shift in our strategic positioning." It suited all of the signatories to AUKUS to exaggerate its importance. For Morrison and Dutton it created the appearance of doing something on national security, for Boris Johnson it was evidence that after Brexit "global Britain" was back, and for Joe Biden it was a counterpoint to the debacle in Kabul.

Shorn of the bravado, apart from the submarines AUKUS does not add up to much more than a continuation of the already intimate collaboration between Australia, the United Kingdom and the United States on security matters, especially signals intelligence. It does not create an obligation in any of the parties to defend the others and is not, as White asserts, "a complete identification of our interests with Washington in dealing with China."

Chinese propaganda has been ready to condemn AUKUS as (yet another) attempt to contain China, but in truth its net effect is more of an own goal. So far AUKUS has:

- done little more than evolve the already close cooperation between the US, UK and Australia;
- seriously undermined the trust France had reposed in both Australia and, more consequentially, the United States;
- humiliated France's "Atlanticists," who support closer ties with the United States, and vindicated those, on the extreme left and right, who contend the "Anglo-Saxons" are utterly untrustworthy;
- ensured Australia's new submarine capabilities will be delayed for at least an additional decade – into the 2040s;
- set back the prospects of closer cooperation between Australia, the United States and France in the Pacific; and, if that wasn't enough,
- created a precedent of transferring weapons-grade uranium to non-nuclear weapons states for the purpose of "naval nuclear propulsion," which is not prohibited under the Non-Proliferation Treaty. This has not only caused considerable concern among our ASEAN neighbours, but will also be used by Iran and other would-be nuclear-weapon states as a precedent to allow them to continue enrichment to weapons-grade levels. (There is a wealth of literature on this issue now: see James Acton's "Why the AUKUS Submarine Deal Is Bad for Nonproliferation – And What to Do About It" and multiple speeches, interviews and papers by University of Texas professor Alan Kuperman, including his May 2022 article for the *Bulletin of the Atomic Scientists*.)

Plenty there to celebrate in Beijing, and a reminder that just because you label something #standinguptoChina doesn't mean you aren't shooting yourself in the foot. Equally, just because Beijing is loudly protesting about AUKUS does not mean that it isn't delighted with the chaotic outcome.

However, when it comes to the history of the acquisition of submarines, White is at his most unreliable. It is true that Tony Abbott was intent on buying submarines from Japan, although he did not share the full extent of his commitments to Japan with all his ministers, let alone the Australian public. However, it was Abbott in February 2015, following the "empty chair" spill, who announced there would be a competitive evaluation process to determine which country we would partner with to build the "future submarine." The countries invited to tender were Japan, France and Germany.

I became prime minister in September 2015 and by April 2016 the unequivocal recommendation from our defence department and expert advisory panel was that we should proceed with the proposal from France's Naval Group (then known as DCNS). This was based on the design of its latest nuclear attack submarine, the Barracuda, now known as the *Suffren* class. White says, "Their bid was extremely expensive – perhaps double the price of the competitors." That is untrue. The costs of all three proposals were comparable. More importantly, the French proposal was head and shoulders above the others and the only one which offered a regionally superior submarine.

France also offered the prospect of transitioning to nuclear propulsion over time, but with low-enriched uranium reactors that do not present the proliferation risks that the weapons-grade uranium used by the US and UK navies does.

White goes on to assert that what really drove the AUKUS submarine move was "the growing awareness that the French project was a debacle, and the ever-increasing desire to align ever closer with Washington."

I cannot speak for Morrison and Dutton's motivations, but it is utterly false to describe the French project (more accurately described as an Australian–French–American collaboration) as a debacle. In fact, as was stated by defence department secretary Greg Moriarty in Senate Estimates, the program was not over-budget and, as revealed in defence department correspondence released under FOI requests, it was progressing well and the proposal from Naval Group for the next phase of work was regarded as "affordable and acceptable." Moriarty assured Rear Admiral Greg Sammut, the CEO of the program, that this good news would be passed on to the French and Australian ministers when they met on 30 August – just two weeks before the Australian government terminated the contract.

White is scathing about the decision by Morrison to acquire nuclear-powered submarines from either the United States or the United Kingdom. I described my own reservations at length in a speech to the National Press Club in September 2021.

As Australia has no nuclear industry, let alone any ability to maintain or sustain a naval nuclear propulsion system, the submarines could not be safely operated other than under the supervision of the US Navy. This means an abandonment of Australian sovereignty.

The singular reason my government, and its predecessors, did not seek to procure nuclear-powered submarines was because it recognised that in the absence of a domestic nuclear industry, we would not be able to exercise sovereign control of such submarines. That was precisely the explanation I gave President Trump when he asked me why we were not acquiring US (as opposed to French) submarines.

The likely candidate is a US *Virginia*-class submarine, which is more than twice the size and with more than twice the ship's company of the *Attack*-class (or *Collins*-class) submarines. It is very questionable whether Australia could afford these submarines, let alone recruit and retain the much larger crews required.

Naval nuclear propulsion does offer greater speed and endurance under water, but the vessels are not as stealthy while submerged as a modern diesel/electric boat. The ideal configuration for our navy would be diesel/electric boats for the shallower waters closer to Australia (such as in the archipelagic regions to our north and east) and nuclear-powered boats for longer transits in the Indian and Pacific oceans.

The upshot of proceeding with the acquisition of *Virginia*-class submarines from the United States will be that we will not be able to deploy our most expensive and lethal military capability without the active involvement of the United States.

So AUKUS as an agreement, absent the submarines, is not of great strategic significance. The engagement of "global Britain" in the Pacific, whatever that means, may well not survive the prime ministership of Boris Johnson. If you want a European, nuclear-weapons state that is a permanent UN Security Council member to partner with in the Pacific, it would make more sense to pick the one that is actually in the Pacific, not the one that withdrew its substantive military forces "east of Suez" more than fifty years ago. And it certainly made no sense at all to choose Britain as a new partner in the Indo-Pacific if the price of doing so was shattering the relationship with France.

At this stage, it may well be too late to restart the *Attack*-class program. While all the intellectual property has been retained, the workforce has been dispersed and would take many months to reassemble. Morrison has likely scuttled that option. The proposition that we could buy an "off-the-shelf" submarine from somebody else overlooks the fact that there is no such thing.

The best option at this stage is to acquire nuclear-powered submarines from France. Its production of six *Suffren*-class boats for the French Navy will be complete by 2030 and it would be feasible for that production line to continue to build six or eight boats for Australia, with one becoming available every two years. The submarines would be a more manageable size and cost. Their reactors would use low-enriched uranium – enriched to about 6 per cent, around the same level used in a civil nuclear reactor to generate electricity but far below the 90 per cent level needed to make a weapon. This would reduce the proliferation issues, and the Lockheed Martin combat management system could be readily integrated – much of that design work had been done for the *Attack*-class. In time, the front half of the boat could be built in Australia, with the back half containing the nuclear propulsion system built in France. This would give us nuclear-powered submarines from the early 2030s – a full decade before the *Virginia*-class.

From a strategic point of view, this would cement a partnership with France, a substantial power in the Indo-Pacific, with nearly two million citizens and extensive territories across both oceans. This strategic partnership, and the trust established between myself and President Macron, was seen as the foundation of France's Indo-Pacific Strategy, launched in Sydney at Garden Island on 2 May 2018 – an "Indo-Pacific axis," in his words. It would not diminish our alliance with the United States – the submarines would be interoperable with the US Navy. The only barrier to this course of action would be politics in Washington and Canberra.

White is very critical of the "small target" strategy of the Labor Opposition in the lead-up to the May 2022 election. On the AUKUS issue he makes a fair point. Morrison gave Labor only twenty-four hours' notice of the deal – despite having undertaken to the White House that the Opposition would be fully briefed and supportive. Labor, recognising the risk of a wedge and being framed by Morrison and his friends in the media as "anti-American" or "Manchurian candidates," chose to go with the flow – sign up to the deal but without any time to receive, let alone consider, a fully detailed briefing. It wasn't edifying, but I can understand the political calculation behind it.

The small target may well have helped Albanese and Labor win the election but it does create a challenge for the new government, which must first and foremost set out all the facts surrounding the submarine issue, including the way in which the decision was taken to terminate the *Attack*-class program, the options that remain available, their cost and timing. It must tell the truth about the consequences of operating submarines with weapons grade uranium–fuelled reactors and explain whether the US Navy will allow those submarines to be operated without any US involvement or supervision.

One of the leading figures in the US administration intimately involved in the AUKUS negotiations has been reported in Europe as having justified the deal as "getting the Australians off the fence. We have them locked in now for the next forty years." Now, knowing the individual involved, I can, just, imagine him saying that in an ebullient way. But of course, Australia was never "on the fence" in the sense of being about to move away from the ANZUS alliance to a non-aligned status which was more accommodating to China. But it is significant that this report is widely believed in Europe, and that the AUKUS submarine deal is seen as an abandonment of Australian sovereignty.

It is noteworthy to recall that in President Macron's speech at Garden Island on 2 May 2018 he spoke of how Australia, through its partnership with France, was developing a wider range of allies, pursuing a policy of sovereign autonomy and not simply relying on the United States. He was quite right; that was precisely my thinking, and my government's strategy.

That is why I often talked about our seeing our region as not simply a series of spokes leading into the imperial capitals of Washington and Beijing, but rather as a mesh where we found our security, as Keating used to say, not *from* Asia but *in* Asia, by building closer ties with our neighbours, whether it be Indonesia, Japan, South Korea, Singapore, India or, indeed, France with its vast Indo-Pacific territories.

Hugh White's bleak realism is as usefully challenging as it is dangerously mistaken, although his warning about not putting all our strategic eggs in one basket is a fair one. However, he is just wrong in saying that Australian foreign policy has been monotonously obedient to, and enthralled by, Washington.

During my own time, I displeased President Obama by not falling into line with his wishes on the treatment of pharmaceuticals in the Trans-Pacific Partnership. With President Trump, of course, we went toe to toe on a refugee deal, as we did on steel tariffs. In both cases our officials would have been happier if I had taken a path of less resistance. Similarly we did not agree to our navy conducting freedom-of-navigation operations within 12 nautical miles of claimed Chinese "islands" in the South China Sea. And perhaps most significantly, when Trump pulled out of the TPP and everyone thought the deal was dead, we persuaded other countries, especially Japan, to stick with the deal and as a result it was revived and concluded without the United States.

Similarly, White complains that Australia has neglected the Pacific and says we must do more than simply tell our Pacific islands neighbours not to deal with China. Well, leaving aside Morrison's shameful diplomatic failure in Solomon Islands over the past few years, our diplomacy in the Pacific has been very active. In my own time we persuaded Solomon Islands not to do a deal with Huawei for an international cable network, not by lecturing them on the evils of communism but by building a cable network ourselves and funding it almost entirely out of our aid budget. We did similar things in PNG and Fiji.

White urges Australia to "stop telling our Southeast Asian neighbours that US primacy is the only path to regional order and start listening to them about how they see China's and India's rises and how they are dealing with them."

In numerous discussions with ASEAN leaders I have never spoken to them in those terms and always sought and listened to their views. Many of my predecessors have done so as well, as have most of our foreign ministers. During my time we stepped up our engagement with ASEAN with new agreements with Singapore, Indonesia and particularly important security assistance in the Philippines. In my experience most ASEAN leaders welcomed a continued American security presence in the region, recognised that China would seek to exert more influence as it became stronger, and saw the United States as a vital counterweight. Hugh White's prediction that America will depart this region and leave it to China would fill almost every nation in ASEAN with dread.

For my own part, I believe the United States will remain engaged in this region for many years to come. The United States is as much a Pacific nation as Australia; it can never responsibly or rationally cede this hemisphere to an unchallenged hegemony of China.

White recommends that Taiwan be abandoned by the United States to Xi Jinping, and that Australia should have nothing whatsoever to do with helping America defend it. But on that basis Ukraine would have been swallowed by Russia, which would now be moving on the Baltic states and on its way to restore the Soviet empire. And if Taiwan were to be overcome, how does that buy peace in our region? One nation after another would acquire nuclear weapons to make itself unassailable. If the risks of nuclear conflict are high today, the withdrawal of the United States in the manner White contemplates would send them sky-high.

The truth is we are living in a time when the pace and scale of change are without precedent. We have to expect, as Margaret Thatcher said, the unexpected. And that means that Australia must have a thoroughly independent foreign policy. The more independent it is, the more influence we have around the world, in our region and indeed in Washington and Beijing. As an ASEAN foreign minister once said to me "If we see you as a rubber stamp for Washington, why would we waste time talking to you? Easier just to talk to head office."

As far as the defence of Australia is concerned, we must be able to defend ourselves and that means that all of our defence capabilities must be sovereign Australian ones, able to be maintained, sustained and deployed by Australia without the approval or supervision of any other nation.

Of course we look to our allies to support us in times of need, as we will support them, but we cannot look out across the decades to come and assume those allies will always be there.

Malcolm Turnbull

SLEEPWALK TO WAR

Correspondence

Kevin Rudd

There seems to be an immutable law of Australian national security policy that the more challenging our external strategic circumstances, the more polarised, polemical and facile the debate becomes.

In the blue corner stands Peter Dutton from the Queensland Far-Right School of International Relations. His view: the more Australia could ingratiate itself with Donald Trump, ignore our immediate region and screech at Beijing every Monday morning, the more Australia's national security would be enhanced.

And in the red corner, Hugh White from the Lord Halifax Appeasement Faction of the Green Left. With supreme self-confidence, White considers America already done for as a regional (and probably global) power; it should "gracefully withdraw" from Asia, leaving the keys for Beijing in the mailbox; and Australia should start chatting to our Marxist-Leninist friends in Beijing about our "role" in the new regional Sinosphere.

On any realist analysis aimed at safeguarding Australia's territorial integrity, political sovereignty and national economic interests, Dutton is as strategically dangerous as White is strategically naive.

Dutton represents the reverse of Theodore Roosevelt's dictum to "speak softly and carry a big stick" – instead, he tramples loudly through the jungle of international relations wielding no stick at all. That he departed office without a single new submarine (or even a contract to build one) after years of fulmination underscored how Morrison's government saw foreign and security policy as little more than the continuation of domestic politics by other means. Nobody, apart from Beijing, took it seriously. Its shallow, shabby effort to discredit its political opponents in a fraudulent khaki election nonetheless had important real-world consequences for China's long-term assessment of Australia as a potentially implacable enemy.

White leans heavily into the winds of political exhaustion, reaction and anxiety fostered by this egregious policy overreach to now paint a simplistic picture of a more benign future under what he accepts as an inevitable Chinese "regional hegemony." A skilled political operator, White adduces selective facts and little reason in reaching this conclusion, but happily smears as "unthinking" anyone who challenges his word as self-appointed prophet of both the anti-American far left and the "never upset Beijing" Rio Tinto far right. It is therefore important to deconstruct both White's analysis of our future strategic environment (whereby almost everything is headed Beijing's way) and his six-point prescription for Australia.

White's bottom-line conclusion, peering through a glass dimly, is that it is game over for America. As evidence, he claims the economic gap between the United States and China is unassailable, that Taiwan is indefensible and that America is domestically ungovernable. He further advances, ex cathedra, that China's projection of power should not cause any real concern for our territorial integrity, political sovereignty or economic interests. America is declining and should withdraw, China will emerge as a regional hegemon, and these fundamentally altered strategic circumstances require an equally fundamental Australian adjustment towards a Whitean form of neutrality.

There are many factual problems with White's intellectually arrogant futurology that demand a factual response. For example, White cites the "simple fact" China's GDP is already larger and growing faster than America's, but doesn't disclose this is based on purchasing power parity (PPP) rather than market exchange rates. This is a big difference: US GDP is 30 per cent larger than China's on market rates, but appears 16 per cent smaller on PPP. Why not acknowledge this important qualification? Because it does not support White's narrative.

A further complication for White's Chinese economic determinism is Xi Jinping's ideological decision since 2017 to take China's economy decisively to the left, radically altering its economic growth model by attacking the private sector in general, and tech, finance and property businesses in particular. Add to this China's rapidly ageing population, contracting workforce, collapsing productivity growth and rolling "zero Covid" lockdowns. Long-held assumptions about Chinese linear economic growth have changed, and debates are erupting among non-partisan economists over what this means for its long-term growth (see, for example, works by Daniel Rosen and the Lowy Institute). But none of these doubts creep into White's essay because, once again, they don't fit his thesis.

Further, on technology, despite unprecedented public investment since 2015 to make China a world leader in all ten critical future technology categories, the evidence of real-world progress is at best mixed. Politically sanctioned state-owned enterprises are crowding out private innovators (particularly in semiconductors, where the United States and its allies, notably Taiwan and South Korea, remain decisively ahead). The core point: the jury is out on who wins the global race for economic and technological pre-eminence between China, and the United States and its closest allies. On current evidence, I'm not prepared to pick. But White breezily assumes it's all over, red rover. Really?

On the military – an equally critical determinant of future great-power status – the jury is also out. White urges Australians to "get real" and abandon the comfortable consensus that "America's position in Asia is invulnerable, that its armed forces are unbeatable, and that its commitment to Asia is unshakable." Wow. Talk about the ultimate straw-man argument. For anyone who witnessed the fall of Saigon in 1975, the invasion of Iraq in 2003 or the reinstallation of the Taliban in 2021, these are not hidden truths. America regularly screws up. We know that. But its military remains the most formidable fighting force on Earth, battle-hardened and constantly modernising its doctrines and weaponry. By contrast, China last fought a major naval battle in 1895, which it lost. And, as the Ukrainians have demonstrated, it is impossible to prejudge the success of a "porcupine strategy" to defend Taiwan against a mainland invasion. Taiwan has 25 million people who have repeatedly told pollsters they would fight to the end for their democracy. Taiwan is already well armed, well trained and has greater capabilities on the way aimed at deterring attack or else fighting a bloody war of attrition. Furthermore, killing hundreds of thousands of Chinese on Taiwan would hardly be politically popular on the mainland. A full-scale maritime invasion would also involve the single biggest amphibious operation since D-Day. So I'd add a note of caution to White's conclusion that conflict over Taiwan would be a lay-down misère for Beijing.

Another tranche of White's argument is that, unlike communist China, the United States is politically divided and shows no appetite for reinvesting in the future pillars of American national power. Meanwhile, neo-isolationists, such as Trump's America-Firsters, stand by to torpedo any consensus. White is correct that US politics is changing fundamentally, in significant part because our very own Citizen Murdoch has fused acute partisan division, the lunatic right and the dynamic that drove the 6 January insurrection into a successful business model for Fox News. But it remains far from clear that US politics are irredeemable. Unlike White, I have lived in the United States for most of the past decade, including through the Trump phenomenon. It is as probable as not that America's democracy, like its economy, will successfully reinvent itself – as it did in 1776, 1812, 1865, 1917, 1932, 1941, 1945 and 1974–75. I'm not prepared to bet the house on it, though White apparently is.

From these unreliable foundations, White advances a six-point strategy to "get out of this mess." Running to eleven pages, this is where dubious analysis degenerates into policy farce. His first three points go to nothing approaching rigorous policy, but rather pop psychology. The first is to "get real about the situation we face … stop underestimating China's power and resolve, and overestimating America's, because a correct assessment of their relative positions is essential." White doesn't explain how his "correct assessment" of China's rising regional power accounts for Korea, Japan and India all turning decisively against China. While ASEAN remains the geopolitical swing state, Beijing's only semi-reliable strategic partners in all of Asia are North Korea, Pakistan and Cambodia.

His second point is to "build a more balanced and realistic view of China" and "keep China's power in proportion." I have been examining Chinese politics and foreign policy for forty years. There have been profound changes under Xi that have turned China politically leftward and moved its nationalism more decisively to the right. My conclusion is that China will be increasingly assertive. Meanwhile, White's "balanced and realistic" analysis is coloured by such bold but unsubstantiated conclusions that Russia will inevitably split from China because of their historical rivalry. He misses that Russia now has nowhere else to turn; that China is very happy with this new dependency; that it suits both parties' strategic interests deeply; and that this is unlikely to change under either Putin or Xi, both of whom plan to remain in office for fifteen more years at least.

The third pillar of the White Doctrine is to "think seriously of war." Some of us lesser mortals, Hugh, do think about these things too. I just wrote an entire book on the subject, titled *The Avoidable War*, which outlines a proposal to do just that through what I call "managed strategic competition" or MSC. It's not rocket science, but has been positively reviewed by the likes of Graham Allison (author of *Essence of Decision* and *Destined for War*), Joseph Nye ("Soft Power" and "Smart Power"), James Stavridis (formerly NATO's supreme commander) and Henry Kissinger. But White fails to take his own advice and, rather than thinking seriously, simply dismisses MSC as unworkable by lazily misrendering its core arguments, probably because they don't suit his case. For example, White falsely describes MSC as a "compromise" proposal for both sides "sharing power" in Asia; in reality, MSC proposes vibrant strategic competition within a set of minimum guardrails to reduce the risk of escalation, crisis, conflict and war. White insists China won't agree to MSC to limit the risk of war by, for example, dialling back its more daring military exercises in the Taiwan Strait, because it wants to change the status quo; but White entirely misses the point that such exercises heighten the risk of stumbling into conflict by mistake. White also criticises MSC for not resolving the "underlying differences" that sustain US–China strategic competition – something MSC explicitly does *not* attempt to do. MSC is designed to reduce the risks of strategic competition escalating into unintended war – not to eliminate strategic competition altogether, which is utterly unrealistic. The only reasonable explanation for White blatantly mischaracterising the core argument of MSC is to dismiss it as an alternative to his own capitulationist approach.

White's fourth pillar is to "talk to America about its future in Asia" and, assuming we are unsatisfied, encourage Washington to abandon Taiwan's democracy to Beijing and "withdraw quickly and gracefully" from Asia. This is perhaps the single most naive element of White's grand schema. What does he imagine the impact would be on US allies globally? Every security guarantee involving America and its allies would be rendered worthless, while democracies as a genus would henceforth be regarded as politically and strategically expendable. Not to mention the real-world political response in the country that, rightly or wrongly, has seen itself as the world's "city on the hill." White's admonition to tell the United States to cut and run is appeasement writ large, politically naive, morally corrupt and with profound geopolitical implications far beyond East Asia if Washington were to concur.

Point five is to recast our diplomacy to be more attentive to our neighbours. This is simply a motherhood statement. Regional political, diplomatic and economic engagement is essential whatever our strategic circumstances. Here, White dances around the bleeding obvious: that Liberal governments have treated most of Asia and the Pacific badly, and Labor governments since H.V. Evatt have done the reverse, as we are seeing once again under Albanese.

The lynchpin of White's six-point plan is the final one: Australia should "start talking seriously to China" about our role in its regional hegemony. But he then slides off this core point after a mere ninety-three words. Talk about what? What White is squeamish about admitting is that this is code for Australia's status under a new *Pax Sinica*. This goes to the heart of Beijing's plan beyond the opaque diplomatic language of "neighbouring states diplomacy," a "community of common destiny" and "win-win cooperation." Despite China's hints of a hardline, Leninist, realist edge (for example, through its recent coercive economic diplomacy against states it disagrees with), we simply do not know what a Sinocentric regional order would look like in practice. And as for White's more immediate suggestion that Australia make concessions to restart bilateral negotiations (because the Chinese are "fundamentally … more important to us than we are to them," and castigating Albanese as "weak" for delegating meetings with Chinese officials to Foreign Minister Wong), this singular piece of advice has already aged poorly. At the time of writing, Wong had already broken the ministerial freeze by meeting her counterpart, Wang Yi, in Bali without a single concession, and with Albanese stating resolutely that "Australia doesn't respond to demands."

In summary, White would bet Australia's entire national security future on what is at best a couple of hunches: first, that China will inevitably prevail over the United States and its allies, and America therefore should seek early terms; and second, that Australia should "talk" to Beijing on what Australia's role in this future Sinosphere should be. White argues both propositions with supreme self-confidence without, to my knowledge, ever having studied or read a word of Chinese, or graduated in Chinese history, or specialised in the Marxist-Leninist doctrines of the Chinese Communist Party. My argument is more modest: simply that the jury is out on White's first proposition, where there is much history still to be written; and the second is a massive poke in the dark, given that the internal planning processes of the CCP on the future of the international order are still unclear. White's written reply to this critique should provide substantial responses to each of these factual challenges, rather than resorting to the usual repertoire of caricature, polemic and diversion.

While these two historical questions are played out, I have argued a different framework for Australia–China relations built on five principles: first, be unapologetic with Beijing that Australia is a democracy that believes in universal human rights grounded in the Universal Declaration, which China has also ratified, and that this will remain a running tension in the relationship; second, our US alliance will remain fundamental because it has added to our national security under multiple strategic scenarios over the past century; third, Australia and China should maximise bilateral economic and people-to-people engagement to the benefit of both countries; fourth, Australia and China should also collaborate at the G20 and all forums of global governance on climate change, pandemic management and global financial stability; and fifth, if we disagree with Beijing, we should do so in partnership with our international friends and allies, rather than flying solo like Morrison and Dutton. Further, we should bring the rhetorical temperature of the relationship down because – despite what Dutton may believe – megaphone diplomacy achieves nothing in foreign policy and (as the last election demonstrates) precious little in domestic politics.

This five-point approach represents a rational middle course between the hairy-chested world according to Peter Dutton and the deeply analytically flawed, brave new world according to Hugh White.

Kevin Rudd

SLEEPWALK TO WAR

Correspondence

Michael J. Green

Hugh White's essay *Sleepwalk to War* starts with a compelling observation about China. "Not since we faced Imperial Japan in the 1940s," he states, "have things been so bad between us and a major Asian power. And this is potentially worse." This jarring but accurate statement is the right starting point for a serious discussion about Australian strategy and managing relations with China and the alliance with the United States. But the essay unfortunately goes on to provide the wrong diagnosis of the problem and then essentially concludes that the best treatment for Australia is pre-emptive strategic euthanasia.

Sleepwalk to War reads like an Australian iteration of the hyper-realism of self-professed American "restrainers" such as John Mearsheimer or Stephen Walt. The balance of power that upsets these authors most is not in the Indo-Pacific, but in Canberra and Washington. Their greatest ire is reserved not for China or Russia, but for their own foreign policy establishments' "alliance back-slapping" and "cringe-makingly sentimental" statements.

It is always fun to critique the bureaucrats, of course, but the attacks would be more convincing if the underlying analysis of the power dynamics in the international system was actually right. The geopolitical competition in the Indo-Pacific is not the simple bipolar contest between China and America that Hugh posits; nor is the world moving towards respective spheres of influence with China at the centre of Asia, as he predicts. The only country in the region that would like this to be so is China, which is why Beijing promotes its own version of Hugh's argument through repetition of Graham Allison's "Thucydides Trap" thesis and offer of a "new model of great power relations," in which the United States would avoid conflict by conceding to Chinese demands in a bipolar condominium that excludes the interests of Australia, Japan and other US allies and partners.

But this is not Athens and Sparta. The regional distribution of power is not bipolar. Instead, the Indo-Pacific region is defined increasingly by a multipolarity in which almost all of the other regional powers greatly prefer the existing US-led rules-based order to Chinese hegemony. To the extent Hugh pays attention to the other players in the system, it is to dismiss them as doomed or feckless. He ignores Japan's growing defence capabilities, jointness with the United States and infrastructure financing (which rivals China's Belt and Road and is much better received); South Korea's recent election of a government much more aligned with US regional strategy; and Europe's harder line on China. He casts India as largely irrelevant because New Delhi is refusing to become a real ally like Australia, when the US strategy was always premised on India not being an ally but a counterweight to China in a multipolar Asia – a reasonable long-term bet considering India's demographic advantage over China.

The diplomacy involved in a multipolar Asia is not always straightforward, to be sure: Southeast Asia and the Pacific will always be porous; India will never be fully aligned; and the architecture of multipolarity will remain fluid and messy and fall short of a convenient collective security arrangement like NATO. But for a realist supposedly preoccupied with the distribution of power, it is a major oversight for Hugh to ignore the growing pushback against China in Tokyo, New Delhi and increasingly Seoul and Brussels. And it would be strategic malpractice for any Australian or US government not to harness this resistance to maintain a favourable balance of power going forward.

Hugh's assertions about the economic power dynamics in China and the United States are also lopsided. Readers should by now be sceptical of the linear projections of Chinese economic dominance that underpin Hugh's geopolitical arguments. As former US Treasury secretary Larry Summers predicted – even before Beijing's self-defeating COVID lockdown, squelching of the private sector and real estate downturn – Chinese growth is reverting to the historical international norm. The United States averaged growth rates of 2.9 per cent from 1979 to 2021 and is projected by most economists to continue that performance in future. China averaged 9.5 per cent from 1979 into the second decade of this century, but now hopes for a 5.5 per cent growth rate that few private economists think is actually achievable (many predict stagflation this year). Even if China surpasses the United States in nominal GDP in the next decade, the next largest economies will still be the United States, India and Japan – collectively larger than China's GDP and none prepared to cede regional economic leadership to Beijing. This is not to argue that the China challenge will solve itself because of China's internal contradictions – its economy and military are huge and the strategic challenge for the rest of us is as real and as perilous as Hugh asserts in the opening of his essay. History suggests an economically stressed China could be even more dangerous for the world. But either way, it is important not to hyperventilate about China's inexorable economic dominance over Asia. That is not how Chinese business leaders privately describe their own projections or why they increasingly seek permanent resident status in Singapore.

In addition to miscasting the material distribution of power, Hugh's essay also misreads American willpower and intentions. His critique of the Obama, Trump and Biden administrations' lurching and uneven efforts to find the right balance of cooperation and competition with China is not entirely unfair. As I described in my own history of US strategy in Asia, *By More Than Providence* (which Hugh kindly cites), the American way of grand strategy is always a messy "meta-process," as one would expect in a system of government designed to reinforce checks and balances. Australia too was uncertain of what the transition from Hu Jintao's China to Xi Jinping's China meant in the years from John Howard to Scott Morrison. Hugh is also right to argue (as I and other American scholars such as Hal Brands and Zack Cooper have) that Washington has left big gaps in its emerging China strategy, including the fundamental question of what "victory" in a strategic competition with China looks like.

But while Hugh gets the faults in the American policy-making process right, he completely misinterprets the historic definition of US strategic interests. George F. Kennan would not have argued that Chinese domination of the Eurasian continent would be acceptable because it is far from the American homeland, as Hugh implies. In fact, Kennan asserted that there are two geographic "strongpoints" that would always remain essential to American security: Western Europe and Japan (and, by extension, the waters of the western Pacific beyond Japan, Taiwan and the Philippines that make up the first island chain). There is still broad consensus in the US strategic community and in Congress that Chinese control of maritime Asia is fundamentally unacceptable – a tradition that did not begin or end with Kennan. China's strategy is clearly premised on domination of the first and second island chains, of course, which puts the US alliance system and Beijing's vision of its security on a collision course. Hugh is right about what is at stake in that sense. But he is wrong to assert that historical American definitions of geopolitical interests in Asia point to a viable accommodation of Chinese dominance of the region. Several opinion polls (Pew, Chicago Council on Global Affairs, CSIS) indicate that the American public gets this and is more willing than ever to defend allies in the Indo-Pacific should it become necessary.

By extension, Hugh draws all the wrong conclusions about the geopolitical significance of Taiwan to US interests. The United States would not be able to brush off a Chinese takeover of Taiwan with skilful reassurance of Japan, as Hugh argues. The reality is that successful Chinese coercion of Taiwan would sever the first island chain, isolate Australia, put Taiwanese semiconductor firm TSMC and the "Ruhr Valley" of advanced semiconductor fabrication under Beijing's control, and force states across the region to choose neutralism or possibly nuclear weapons to survive in the new environment.

But neither does Beijing have clear options to take Taiwan, as Hugh asserts. It would not be "easy for China to control the seas off Taiwan" for an invasion. While a Taiwan fight would be dangerous for surface combatants on all sides, the US Navy maintains a significant edge in undersea warfare that would make amphibious operations highly perilous for the PLA. Ukraine's success against the Russian Navy in the Black Sea illustrates how much Taiwan could further complicate Chinese military planning with the introduction of more anti-ship missiles: a capability now at the top of Taipei's shopping list. In short, it has become harder for the United States to execute its traditional plans for the defence of Taiwan, but Beijing hardly has an easy path of its own to victory. The unprecedented unity of US global alliances in response to Putin's attack on Ukraine will further complicate Chinese assumptions about the use of force against Taiwan: Europe may not be neutral in Asian crises after all, as Beijing clearly assumed for years. That does not mean NATO sends warships, but there are now clearer geopolitical and economic costs to aggression. The bottom line is that deterrence and peace in the Taiwan Strait are still achievable, while pre-emptive surrender of Taiwan is neither necessary nor a reliable path to lasting peace.

The most surprising aspect of Hugh's essay to me as an American is the curiously apathetic definition of Australia's core values and interests. There may be an appetite in some corners for critiquing bureaucrats in Canberra or Washington, but would there really be political support in Australia for accepting the implications of Chinese hegemonic dominance of the Indo-Pacific? Is that the "China choice" Australians would make? Would they be prepared to curtail their free speech, as Beijing is already demanding, or to accept the odious apparatus of China's high-tech surveillance state or PLA military bases in their immediate region? It is difficult to see any democratic society signing up for such a future – particularly when predictions of Chinese dominance and American retreat are built on such flimsy analytical scaffolding.

One thing Hugh gets absolutely right is how much influence Australia has in Washington. As he notes, the strategic community on Asia policy in DC is pretty small (I should know, I was part of it) and also very impressionable (see earlier parenthetical comment). If there are good ideas from trusted partners like Australia, they go right to the top. That is particularly true today, when the Congress and the Biden administration put such heavy emphasis on alliances and when Americans (especially younger Americans) are more positively disposed towards allies in polling than ever. But Hugh is wrong when he asserts that Australian officials just use that influence to cheer for whatever America wants. That was never my experience in my time in the Pentagon, the White House, or in think-tanks in DC. Australian officials may close ranks with the United States in public, but they don't cheerlead in private. More often, they join forces with Japan or Britain to push the US system towards smarter policies. Sometimes they fail, but more often they succeed. AUKUS, the White House Indo-Pacific Strategy with its emphasis on engaging Southeast Asia, and the renewed US commitment to the Pacific Islands are just three recent examples of direct Australian influence on US strategy. I suspect that if the Australian embassy followed Hugh's advice and went to President Biden to say, "You can't win, best to turn the place over to China before it's too late," the meeting would not go well and Australian strategic influence in Washington and by extension the region would start to plummet. But since no Australian government on the horizon is likely to do that, I do not lose much sleep over that scenario.

What Australia should do with its influence is continue shaping American strategy towards China, not trying to break it. Hugh notes that the Biden administration has yet to define what victory looks like in the competition with China. Fair point. Australia should push the Biden administration to think over the horizon to a regional order that rests on a more sustainable equilibrium with Beijing. That starts with shoring up a favourable balance of power, enhancing deterrence, blunting dangerous Chinese initiatives and investing in the resilience of smaller states in the region. But if the goal is to find acceptable terms for less dangerous and more productive relations with China down the road, then the United States should be more focused on economic statecraft that can provide leverage over China's treatment of investors and trading partners, rather than just looking at ways to decouple. In that regard, the Indo-Pacific Economic Framework is still a very thin reed compared with the Trans-Pacific Partnership, and Australia and other allies are right to push Washington to do more to shape regional economic rules. Along the same lines, the Biden administration would do well to reintroduce the kind of strategic dialogue with Beijing that Bob Zoellick in the Bush administration and Hillary Clinton in the Obama administration sustained with key players like State Counselor Dai Bingguo. Xi's opaque and authoritarian leadership style makes this harder but it is no less important. In some ways Washington is still in the John Foster Dulles stage of competition and will sooner or later have to get to the JFK stage, when tough-minded but serious dialogue channels were established with Moscow – and this time preferably not after a Cuban missile crisis. (The administration has tried to establish transparency and guardrails around high-risk areas, such as nuclear weapons, but these talks have been aimed at making geopolitical competition less dangerous rather than finding a sustainable strategic equilibrium.) So yes, there are shortcomings in the US strategic approach where quiet prodding by close allies can help – as it often has in the past.

A balanced assessment of power and purpose in the Indo-Pacific would highlight for Australian policy-makers when to invest in jointness and interoperability with the United States, when to support American resolve, when to partner with Japan or others, and when to hedge. It would also highlight where pushback and risk are necessary with China, and where reassurance and even cooperation might be possible. There is no binary "China choice." Instead, there are dozens if not hundreds of smaller choices that strategists and policy-makers must make to protect Australian interests – just as there are in the United States. Fortunately, a balanced assessment of the strategic dynamics of the Indo-Pacific will lead us to the same conclusions in almost every case – and with a growing number of like-minded allies and partners along the way.

So kudos to Hugh for shaking things up as always. There is urgency, as he notes. There are also many big and hard decisions ahead. But the basic consensus behind current Australian and American grand strategy is founded on a more nuanced and realistic assessment of the international system and the relative balance of power than offered in the polemical pages of *Sleepwalk to War*.

Michael J. Green

SLEEPWALK TO WAR

Correspondence

Kishore Mahbubani

A prophet, they say, is never recognised in his time. This may well be the fate of Hugh White. For decades, he has been accurately warning that the geopolitical environment around Australia has changed and will continue to change. Curiously, even though many of his warnings have come true, his voice hasn't been heeded. Indeed, I have met many Australians who dismiss his work by saying, "Oh, that's Hugh White."

Many of the opponents and detractors of Hugh White claim that they are the hard-headed and tough-minded "realists." Actually, their heads are full of intellectual mush as they ignore two critical geopolitical realities. First, geography is destiny. If, as White predicts, China becomes the number-one power in the world and America becomes number two and the rest of Asia adapts intelligently and pragmatically, Australia will be left isolated in its own geographical region. As White says, "We'd face harsher diplomatic isolation, fewer economic opportunities and more military pressure from Beijing, and less support and cooperation from our more prudent neighbours." In short, Australia could functionally become the Cuba of Asia. The second geopolitical reality that the right-wing hawks ignore is that great powers will not set aside their own national interests to save smaller ally states, even those who share the same cultural skin. White is therefore right to emphasise that Australia has been abandoned before. As White says, "Australia is no stranger to alliance failure, as Morrison should have recalled before talking of a 'forever partnership' with the United Kingdom. Our first great alliance failed in 1941, at what was, until now, the most perilous moment of our history." As White warns, 1941 could happen again for Australia.

One of the biggest strengths of this latest Quarterly Essay by Hugh White is its accurate and insightful analysis of the new geopolitical realities of East Asia, driven primarily by the return of China as one of the biggest economies of the world. Few Australians seem to be aware of a simple fact that White highlights in his first paragraph: "Today China's economy is 19 per cent of global GDP and America's is 16 per cent. By 2035, China will be at 24 per cent and America just 14 per cent."

Curiously, in the early decades of China's rise, Australia adapted intelligently and pragmatically to this new geopolitical environment. Indeed, Gough Whitlam, Bob Hawke and Paul Keating forged good ties with their Chinese counterparts. Even as late as John Howard, China was managed carefully and sensitively by Australia. In 1996, Howard told Jiang Zemin that Australia's alliance with America was sacrosanct, but that nothing Australia did as a US ally would be directed against China. Sadly, all these decades of careful management of China were washed away when Malcolm Turnbull and Scott Morrison came to power. Future historians will truly marvel that Australia decided to take on China just as America had elected the most unreliable (to its allies) administration in its history: the Trump administration. Indeed, Morrison and his government tried to out-Trump Trump. As White says, "This is the spirit in which [Morrison] refused even to meet China's newly arrived ambassador in Canberra." Morrison and his team were probably unaware that Beijing has a long memory.

It was unwise for the Morrison government to align itself with the Trump administration when it launched a geopolitical contest against China without first working out a thoughtful and comprehensive long-term strategy to ensure that America would win. As White says, "Competing with China for primacy in East Asia is by far the most serious strategic commitment America has undertaken since the Cold War. And yet Washington has launched into it with no clear idea of what would count as winning, how it could be won, how much it will cost and why winning really matters." Indeed, this is the key message of my book *Has China Won?* – that America has no long-term strategy for managing the competition with China. And, as I document in the book, this insight was personally given to me by Henry Kissinger.

One of the wisest pieces of advice that White gives to his fellow Australians is the following: "We should do our due diligence and decide for ourselves if what Washington is saying or doing really stacks up and makes sense. And the closer we look, the worse things appear. The problems start with the most fundamental question: what exactly is Washington trying to achieve?"

Indeed, as I am a friend of America, this is the most basic question I ask my American friends: if all the policies of the Trump and Biden administrations succeed, what will America have achieved? Here are some possible answers: isolate China? Overthrow the Chinese Communist Party? Stop China from becoming the number-one economic power in the world? Even a short list like this makes it clear that America's goals towards China are not clear. White declares that Australians indulge in a "cringe-makingly sentimental and grossly ahistorical talk of our US alliance." This may explain why Australia unthinkingly follows American policy, even if the goals are unclear.

Another great strength of this essay is White's withering and devastating descriptions of the two latest initiatives taken by Australia to counter-balance China: the Quad and AUKUS. As White says, "Washington talks a lot about the Quad – the grouping of India, Japan, Australia and America – as a highly effective counter to China's bid for regional leadership. It is hard to see why, because the Quad does not actually do anything except meet." However, while the Quad may not do much good, it also doesn't do much harm to Australia. By contrast, AUKUS could do Australia much harm. By acquiring nuclear submarines to challenge China's navy, Australia is inserting itself into the front line in a potential nuclear war between China and America. As White says, clearly and bluntly, "All this – the complacency, the incompetence, the illusions – came together in the proposal to acquire nuclear-powered submarines under AUKUS." White could have added that AUKUS also undermined Australia's nuclear non-proliferation credentials. And it also insulted and alienated its largest immediate neighbour, Indonesia, with this AUKUS move.

While I agree a lot with what White says in this essay, I have one major point of disagreement. White is absolutely convinced that China is determined to push America out of East Asia. As he says, "That is what China is trying to do in East Asia today. It aims to assert its place as the region's primary power, and undermine America's position, by showing that it is willing to go to war to push America out of East Asia and that America is not willing to go to war to stop it." The great strength that China's leaders have – as Kissinger documents in his book *On China* – is that they are pragmatic realists. It's vital to note here that the current Sino–American geopolitical contest was started by America, not China. China is clearly pushing for more geopolitical space for itself. But it is willing to share geopolitical space with America as long as America doesn't undermine any vital Chinese interest, such as by advocating for independence for Taiwan.

Indeed, this is the win-win strategy that the ASEAN states are pushing for. They have made it clear, as White confirms, that they don't want to take sides: they want good relations with both America and China. To have good relations with both also means that ASEAN wants America to retain its presence in East Asia. However, they want America to retain a thoughtful and sensitive presence in the region, not the clumsy presence of the Trump administration (with the support of the Morrison government).

At the end of the day, the wisest thing that any Australian government could do is to get the country's geographically isolated, predominantly Western population of 25 million to align itself with the win-win strategy of ASEAN towards managing the Sino–American contest. This is the argument I put across in an essay in the July 2022 issue of *Australian Foreign Affairs*.

If Australia steers towards a greater alignment with the ASEAN position, it could play a useful bridging role between Beijing and Washington, DC. The greatest geopolitical asset Australia has is that it's trusted in Washington. And, as White correctly asserts, American foreign policy is made by a small group of people. As he says, "The essentials of US foreign policy have long been deeply bipartisan, and there has always been a lot of consensus among the tight-knit group of people who work on these issues as they move between universities, think-tanks, congressional staff jobs and official positions in Washington." Australia is trusted by this "tight-knit group." It should persuade them of the wisdom of the ASEAN position that Australia can support. And if Australia does this, it will avoid many of the dangers White warns about. It's time for Canberra to heed its best prophetic voice, that of Hugh White.

Kishore Mahbubani

SLEEPWALK TO WAR

Correspondence

Sam Roggeveen

From the publication of his 2010 Quarterly Essay, *Power Shift*, to the release of his latest, *Sleepwalk to War*, Hugh White's body of work on the consequences of China's rise has generated a mountain of commentary and criticism. Yet remarkably, none of it has laid a glove on his most important claim: that America's overall security is *not* threatened by China's ascent to leadership in East Asia.

If White is correct on this point, it suggests that every statement made by every US administration about the importance of Asia to American security and economic wellbeing, every reassurance to friends and allies in the region that America can only be secure if Asia is secure, is built on sand.

To my knowledge, no one in the Australian security commentariat, or among national security leaders in our two major parties, has directly taken on this crucial idea. White's critics often complain that he has been repeating himself for over a decade. Yet that leaves them no excuse. They should have rebutted him by now.

I don't think we can conclude that silence implies assent. Rather, silence is a form of avoidance because White's conclusion is just too uncomfortable. Australia is betting its future security on the proposition that Asia is critical to the United States, and that therefore the United States will be prepared to secure a favourable order in Asia, even if it means fighting China. White overturns this assumption. He argues that America's security interests in Asia are not vital, and certainly not important enough to risk a catastrophic war with China.

That's a radical enough conclusion, with consequences for Australia that ought to be exercising the minds of our decision-makers. Unfortunately, this government is seemingly no more ready than the last to entertain any limits to what it insists on calling the "unbreakable alliance," as if such a thing ever existed in history. Yet in *Sleepwalk to War*, White goes further still, when he describes what comes after American leadership in Asia. He says, "it is hard to see what could stop China dominating East Asia and the Western Pacific. No other country in the region has either the power or the disposition to resist it."

This is where White leaves room for debate. His use of the term "dominance" is not quite consistent throughout the essay. At some points "dominance" seems highly coercive. For instance, White says that to really threaten America, China would have to dominate Eurasia first: "Only then would it command a material resource base big enough to overwhelm American conventional defences and – just conceivably – overmatch and neutralise its nuclear forces. And only then would it be free of rivals closer to home, which would allow it to focus its power on America."

So "domination" here refers to a great power's ability to agglomerate the resources of the states which it dominates, and then direct this combined force at a rival. It also implies that the dominant power can impose its foreign policy goals on subordinate states. This would be something akin to the Soviet Union's position vis-à-vis the smaller Warsaw Pact countries.

But White also says: "India will dominate South Asia and the Indian Ocean, and China will dominate East Asia and the Western Pacific. Each of them will be strong enough to deter the other from seriously interfering in its sphere of influence."

Here we might interpret White as saying that to dominate a region is to exercise a sphere of influence over it. But a "sphere of influence" is commonly defined as being looser and less intrusive than "dominance." As White points out, Australia has traditionally exercised a sphere of influence in the Pacific, as does the United States in Latin America. Where a major power boasts a sphere of influence, it can exercise authority due to its economic and military weight. It can also exclude other great powers from exerting influence within the sphere. Yet as traditionally defined, a sphere of influence does not allow the leading power to appropriate the military, diplomatic and economic resources of the countries under their tutelage to further their own foreign policy ambitions.

Is Chinese "dominance" of East Asia likely by the first, stronger, definition? It is not the present reality, even for North Korea, China's only formal ally. Perhaps weaker Southeast Asian states such as Laos, Cambodia and Myanmar will fall under China's direct control (though if they ever do, they will become a drain on Chinese power rather than add to it). China is not likely to impose direct Soviet-like control over bigger Southeast Asian countries, and for powers such as Japan, South Korea, Indonesia and Australia it is out of the question unless China physically conquers them first.

I would argue that even the latter, weaker, definition of "dominance" does not fully describe Asia's likely future under Chinese leadership. True, we can already see the makings of a Chinese sphere of influence in its relations with smaller Southeast Asian neighbours. Others may slip further into China's orbit and away from the United States; the Philippines and Thailand look particularly vulnerable.

But beyond that, the task will be challenging for China because maintaining a sphere of influence over maritime Asia requires enormous resources – primarily a huge navy, preferably with a handful of well-located foreign bases to support it. Of course, China has a big navy, and nobody can stop it from getting much bigger still. But as White himself has argued forcefully on other occasions, in the maritime realm, the advantage rests with the side trying to prevent an adversary from imposing dominance.

This is especially true over long distances, which make it difficult to project sustained naval power. Smaller countries can concentrate their lesser defence resources near their coast, with the result that even much bigger navies can have their power blunted just enough that the smaller state never needs to submit to the great power's authority.

Distance is not the only constraint. Even at a slight geographical remove, smaller powers have options because of the inherent limitations of navies. For instance, White says, "Taiwan cannot realistically expect to defend itself from China." But I would argue it is still too early for such a stark conclusion. Even under the imbalance of forces that exists today, Taiwan has some hope of repelling a Chinese invasion because, in the missile age, military operations involving large surface fleets are incredibly risky, even over short distances. Taiwan is able to impose high costs on China by targeting the ships it needs to mount an invasion. If Taiwan spent more than its current 2 per cent of GDP on defence and sharpened its focus on the so-called "porcupine strategy" (small, agile forces rather than ships, tanks and fast jets), it could set Beijing's ambitions back by years.

Still, let's assume Taiwan is eventually retaken by China. White says this will be a disaster for America's regional alliance structure, which "will crumble" as a result. Again, this seems too stark. It is equally plausible that Japan, South Korea and Australia will breathe a quiet sigh of relief that the United States has conserved its military resources rather than expended them defending Taiwan. Besides, what's the alternative for America's allies? They would need to declare that it is no longer reliable, politely kick US troops out of their countries and then build up their own military forces, including with nuclear weapons. That's much harder than maintaining the status quo.

To return to where we began, none of this is to disagree with White's claim that American resolve in East Asia is eroding and unlikely to recover. The United States faces a highly motivated and well-resourced China, and America's own security interests in the region are not vital enough to justify taking on such a big rival.

But White paints American resolve as a quickly diminishing resource. In fact, he says it could be exhausted at a stroke if Taiwan falls. My response is that for each setback, there is a fallback. China's assertion of hegemony over the South China Sea was a setback, yet American resolve and the US alliance system did not crumble. Nor are they likely to crumble if Taiwan falls.

To be clear, I'm not saying that the United States will transition from a dominant power to a balancing power in East Asia. White argues convincingly that it wouldn't gain much from such an arrangement. If it is self-aware enough to recognise that its vital interests are not threatened by China, then settling for a lesser security role in East Asia is no more attractive than having no role at all. Rather, I would argue that residual American resolve can delay Chinese dominance indefinitely. Japan, South Korea and Australia have strong political and bureaucratic incentives to hold on to their alliances, and America's other partners in the region also want it to stay. On the US side, there is simply no political or bureaucratic constituency for withdrawal from East Asia. Even after a viscerally anti-alliance president came to office in 2016, America's military footprint in Asia did not change.

White would presumably reply that simply maintaining alliance arrangements is not in itself a demonstration of American resolve. To show that it really is committed to competing with China, the United States must massively up its military game in East Asia. He is right. America has been standing pat in East Asia since the end of the Cold War, and although no US administration will ever admit it, this is a de facto decision to go into relative decline. Allies and adversaries recognise this for what it is – an erosion of American resolve.

But America's military presence in Asia, particularly its marines and navy in Japan (55,000 military personnel plus a permanently stationed aircraft carrier), will remain a potent force. Even if this force is outmatched by China in future, it will act as a "trip-wire" whose destruction could prompt the United States to use nuclear weapons in retaliation. As White reminds us, nuclear weapons cast a dark shadow over the US–China contest. While the chance of nuclear use is small, that slight possibility is tremendously significant because the consequences will be so cataclysmic. This low-risk/high-consequence dynamic works against a dramatic transition away from US power because although China may well believe American resolve is eroding, it cannot afford to make risky bets on that belief – the consequences of being wrong are too high. Hence even a lukewarm US commitment to its Asian allies can constrain China.

There is one more extenuating factor. If, as now seems likely, China's economy grows more slowly than previously forecast, we might never see clear daylight between the United States and China in terms of their national power. Recent Lowy Institute research suggests they will remain roughly equal for the indefinite future, which makes China's task of presenting itself as overwhelmingly the leading power in East Asia that much harder.

Again, this will not affect the ultimate transition away from US leadership in East Asia, but it will extend America's horizon. And when the curtain finally falls on the age of American leadership in East Asia, the region stands a good chance of being able to prevent a new era of Chinese dominance.

Sam Roggeveen

Correspondence

Peter Varghese

Hugh White's latest Quarterly Essay is a forensic, clear-eyed and courageous revisiting of the foundations of Australian strategic and foreign policy. Even if you do not agree with his conclusions, Hugh asks the right questions.

His analysis is radical in the true sense of the word: he goes to the root of the issues. And while much of what he concludes is compelling, there are three issues on which I take a somewhat different view.

First, I think he is too stark on a US retreat from the region. It is unlikely, in my view, that America's choice will be as binary as lead or leave. The country is intent on preserving its primacy, but the paradox of US strategy is that retaining primacy will ultimately mean constructing a new strategic equilibrium in the Indo-Pacific, one that involves a more traditional balance of power in which the United States would be but one, albeit powerful, player. That is what the Quad really represents. It is an implicit acceptance that America alone may not be able to match China, but that with others it most certainly can. It is a sublimation of US primacy. But even in a post-primacy world, the United States will retain very significant strategic and economic interests in the Indo-Pacific which will keep it engaged there, unless of course a nuclear war makes all this academic.

Hugh would likely argue that China will eventually force the United States to withdraw from the region because that is what Chinese primacy demands. But that is an overly narrow view of primacy, and I think China neither expects a complete US withdrawal nor is it likely to press until it is achieved. China wants a return to the Middle Kingdom where harmony was hierarchy with China at the top and an expectation that all other states would pre-emptively concede the primacy of China's core interests. If China can secure this it may be willing to live with a US presence that is short of primacy, just as America is currently willing to live with a Chinese strategic presence in East Asia that is short of primacy. Strategic positioning may well be a zero-sum game, but that does not require the United States to go to zero if China succeeds in becoming the predominant power.

Second, Hugh both overestimates and underestimates India's position. I agree that India will want a sphere of influence in South Asia and the Indian Ocean. India will be tenacious in pursuing the first and ultimately unsuccessful in pursuing the second, not only because neither China nor the United States will concede primacy over the Indian Ocean, but also because India will not have the economic or strategic heft over the next few decades to impose its primacy.

One of the features of a multipolar strategic environment, which is where we are heading, is that primacy, by definition, becomes a much more problematic concept. Real primacy means that you are stronger than the aggregate strategic weight of all those who oppose your primacy and I doubt that India can achieve this in the Indian Ocean, just as I doubt that China can achieve it in the Asia-Pacific. It is one thing to be the strongest single power, but quite another to be the hegemon.

Nor will India be relaxed about conceding primacy to China in East Asia, although it may not be able to prevent it. India's economic interests in East Asia will only grow and its strategic relationship with China will become essentially competitive. That is why I am more convinced than Hugh about the validity of the Indo-Pacific framework. It makes little sense to put China and India in separate strategic systems when in the future each will see the other as a primary strategic point of reference. This competitive dynamic will apply across East Asia and the Indian Ocean and will not, as Hugh would have it, be confined to the boundary between South Asia and East Asia.

It is true that India has a substantially opportunistic view of the Quad, but then so do all the Quad members in their own way: a case of same bed, different dreams. And to the extent that the Quad is presented as a spear carrier for democracy, it will have to wrestle with an India which will stay democratic but could well see a Hindu nationalist agenda corrode its secular liberal-democratic character.

Third, Hugh downplays the reality that China is now itself heading in a very uncertain direction. Xi has made some spectacularly bad calls in the cause of party authority. He has reasserted state control of the economy, which can only lead to slower growth. His "wolf warrior diplomacy," whatever domestic returns it delivers, has failed as foreign policy and will have economic consequences, as evidenced by the caution about new foreign investments in China. This is all a result of Xi's absolute determination to ensure party control over everything, but in doing so he is causing an economic slowdown that will challenge the monopoly power of the party. This is a very different set of triggers to the wishful thinking behind the "coming China collapse" theories of the past, and at the very least they should cause us to be more sceptical than we otherwise might be about projections of China's economic growth.

Hugh's most significant insight is our urgent need for a defence force capable of defending our continent without the combat assistance of the United States. This builds on his carefully argued book about how we can do this at an increased but still manageable cost.

We must bury the policy of forward defence once and for all. As long as it sits unexorcised in the background of our defence thinking, we will never shed our ambivalence about whether we can protect our continent without relying on the US cavalry. The point here is not that the United States is unreliable or that the alliance should be abandoned. Neither is true. But ultimately we need to rely on ourselves. The alliance can help us do that, but it cannot do it for us. Australians must overcome the deep-seated belief that we are incapable of defending ourselves. As a G20 economy with a continental geography and the advantages of both distance and alliance-enabled access to advanced defence technologies and platforms, we should have more confidence in ourselves. We are not a lonely country, but we will have to do more to make our own way in a much more complicated world. That should be the starting point of Australian defence and foreign policy.

Peter Varghese

Rory Medcalf

Strategic analysis can be a weird game. With incomplete information, in a haze of uncertainty, you are expected to reach durable conclusions about the interplay of power, people and events, their impact on national interests, and options for sound policy.

There are several ways to play. The most frustrating is the endless hedge of discussion and description, without an actual attempt to guide strategy: matters could go this way, or that; we lack a full dataset (and always will, since this is about the future, not just history); so better to be hesitant than wrong. Leaders shun such stuff. Foreign Minister Penny Wong openly laments commentary that merely "admires the problem."

Rarer is the effort to strike a fine balance of evidence, plausible judgments and practical implications for decision-makers. Proffer conclusions, by all means, but temper with analytic humility. Concede the limits of your information and method, recognise what you may have got wrong in the past, be prepared to change your mind and avoid the temptation to score points. It should be about the community of experts helping government get the best estimate. That's how good assessment works in the intelligence world. It's a pity that public discourse too often responds to other and somewhat perverse incentives: the reward is less for being useful than for product differentiation.

I've admired my ANU colleague Professor Hugh White for decades: his singular intellectual style, public profile (such that many mistakenly assume he speaks for Australia), unorthodox career, generous mentorship of next-generation thinkers, sharp good humour, even his zeal. He is a past master of the strategic analysis game. But he insists on playing it just one narrow way – his own, derived from his training in philosophy and winner-takes-all Oxford debating. And, sadly, his new Quarterly Essay maintains the cage.

True to the essay's title, *Sleepwalk to War*, Hugh's is a mesmerising approach. It's a kind of syllogistic hypnosis, using superbly readable prose to generate camouflage that looks like free and open debate. That sounds uncharitable. But my frustration comes from forever hoping for more: waiting through several essays and books now for Professor White to engage on terms wider than those he rigidly sets (always the same) at the outset of each foray. That, of course, would make for a very different intellectual expedition, one where the end – China wins, America loses, Australia needs to change drastically before it's too late, and anyway it's probably too late – is not preordained. In this ritualised tragedy, the author's argument always triumphs. But the denouement feels less like the outcome of an exhaustive and evidence-rich contest of ideas and more like the imagined acme of Chinese strategy: winning without fighting.

Despite the obligatory early reference to a pat economic projection (that China will overtake America as world's largest economy), and various admissions that we need to consider China's power-play in wider contexts, the essay is really a self-contained drama with few protagonists, dimensions and moving parts. It's primarily about conventional and nuclear military confrontation between China and the United States in East Asia, principally over the status of Taiwan, the risks and projected outcome of war, and the decisions this forces on Australia. This is interspersed with a lot of virtuous throat-clearing about Canberra's alleged missteps in China policy over many years, a critique of the AUKUS technology-sharing agreement and a selective tour of global and regional security dynamics, but all to reinforce the headline argument: that, if we are to live with a powerful China, we must turn our statecraft towards urging America to back off. This means – and Hugh cannot be accused of lacking clarity here – "abandoning Taiwan to Beijing." This line is so thunderous, it may paradoxically lull readers into thinking they're wide awake and alert to all realities, rather than dazed by a false dichotomy.

Hugh aims to provoke, and he does. Other correspondents will no doubt elaborate on the awful implications of such anticipatory capitulation – surrendering a self-ruled, Australia-sized community at the heart of Asia to a fate worse than Hong Kong's, demolishing the most successful democratic endeavour in the history of Chinese civilisation and the most robust young democracy in the Indo-Pacific. Hugh's rejoinder is that, while this may not be pleasant, it beats nuclear war. This computes in the parameters of his self-structured debate, but it ignores all plausible futures short of unlimited war. If you accept that, in the years ahead, Beijing is more likely to launch campaigns of extreme pressure than do-or-die invasion (and that any planned invasion would be preceded by a rising tempo of threats and coercion), then we need to hear also about how to counter and deter China in that vast grey zone. Hugh's commitment to peace is admirable, and his point that America is underinvesting in front-line conventional forces is well made, but this does not mean Beijing is poised to risk doing battle with them. A counsel of despair can also be an invitation to aggression – and overlook that the loss of Taiwan could prove the beginning, not the end, of a perilous struggle for security in Asia, not least in the view from Tokyo.

China doesn't want war, as Hugh acknowledges, and would much prefer a bloodless victory. For Australia, America, Japan and a range of other prospective partners, sensible policy advice therefore would be to understand Beijing's coercive playbook and explore every avenue of preparedness and deterrence. Well before it contemplates total war, China is likely to consider economic sanctions, maritime blockades, political interference, cyberattacks, sabotage of critical infrastructure, disinformation, intimidating military exercises, incursions and seizure of outlying islands. All of these steps are feasible; some are already being tried. They exist in a space of contingency, where matters could go either way: they could be discouraged, even deterred, by a combination of military, economic, cyber, intelligence and diplomatic measures. Or they could bring risks of escalation and damage to the global economy and its technology supply chains, in which Taiwan plays an integral part. But this spectrum of potential Chinese action also widens the range of prospective countermeasures by the many nations wanting to preserve the status quo. These could involve increasing support to Taiwan as an advanced economy and a durable democracy located close to vital international sea lanes, without necessarily crossing thresholds to state recognition.

Even an imminent or limited Taiwan conflict would have dire economic consequences for Australia and globally (as our iron-ore miners privately know, and many corporations worldwide are beginning to wargame). One of the many lessons from Ukraine is the danger of economic reliance providing asymmetric leverage to an authoritarian aggressor. A fruitful avenue for new policy thinking is not only how to wean oneself off such dangerous dependence, but how to begin turning the tables. If Beijing's Taiwan threats jeopardise the international economic order on which China's internal stability depends, then it makes sense to begin mapping the collective geoeconomic leverage of democratic states and signalling how this could be brought to bear. This is a conversation that has begun in America, Japan and, crucially, even in Europe (including Germany) – whose investment, technology and markets China needs more than the other way around. If a Taiwan conflict is going to destroy business as usual – and it surely would – then what's to lose from warning about that up-front and weaponising that fact as a form of deterrence? This geoeconomic dimension may seem peripheral to Hugh's thesis, and may matter less if the shooting starts, but to ignore it entirely is to miss an opportunity for policy advice more realistic and nuanced than simply "abandon Taiwan."

And geoeconomics is hardly the only vital piece of context missing or out of place in the unsettling dream world of *Sleepwalk*. Nations are not billiard balls, responding identically and predictably to the laws of physics: if they were, then Ukraine would have surrendered by day three; Japan, Vietnam, the Philippines and India would long ago have conceded their contested boundaries to China; and Canberra would have meekly accepted the fourteen points accompanying Beijing's economic coercion. Internal dynamics, leadership, risk calculations, events, national identity and public mood all matter. So it is disappointing how little attention the essay pays to what goes on inside China – though surely everything else follows from this.

There's understandable reference to the troubled state of American politics, and a dismissal of the Taiwanese people's will to fight, yet almost nothing about the internal challenges and attitudes of Chinese society, other than the uncritical assertion that primacy or regional leadership is "as dear to China's people as it is to their leaders" – implying that they are universally ready for total war in this cause. This does a disservice to the complexity of what China's people and the Communist Party must face. Development and stability are still compelling national priorities. Yet these must now be achieved with a slowing economy, a rapidly ageing society without a safety net, growing mistrust of China across much of the world, pollution and resource pressures, rolling debt crises, constant suppression of diverse springs of dissent, patterns of political and professional disengagement among youth, and a still-deferred reckoning with the impact of the COVID-19 pandemic. Extreme nationalism spilling into military aggression may be an insecure Xi's circuit-breaker for such internal trouble – or may make China's predicament worse. We simply don't know, though we do know the enormous lengths to which the Communist Party's propaganda machine goes to insist that China owns the future. Yet we are asked to believe that the Chinese people are more than ready to leap over decades of restraint from almost any use of external armed force to risk everything – including generations of economic wellbeing – on a sudden willingness to wage nuclear war, and therefore strategically it's game over.

There's likewise a frustrating selectivity in the essay with evidence when it comes to the crucial questions of Australian and American objectives. We are told Washington is incapable of making Asia policy in any terms other than seeking primacy, even though it is acknowledged that some leading strategic thinkers on both sides of US politics are starting to explore more realistic alternatives. And we are told Australia's entire policy-making elite has timidly put the nation's fate in American hands – even though so many of the decisions that have upset China in recent years (such as the Quad and the bolstering of domestic security) can be read credibly as efforts to diversify our partnerships and do more for our own protection. It's baffling how wilfully the essay jumbles the timeline of Australia–China relations (during, before and after the reality check of the Turnbull years). It's easy to disprove the claim that Australian policy was essentially about impressing and following America. Indeed, Australia was the pioneer on many of the issues Hugh refers to; China knows this, and has said as much, which helps explain its bullying. The first round of the Sam Dastyari affair, which signalled the start of Australian pushback against Chinese Communist Party interference, occurred months *before* the election of Trump – who initially had no wish to pressure allies on China in any case.

The essay is also curiously uneven in the way it treats regional and global settings, as if these are painted opera scenery to be moved around as fits the unfolding plot. On the one hand, we are told China wants primacy in East Asia but is content to leave its hands off the Indian Ocean (and by extension South Asia and Africa), and will fail – thanks to Indian, Russian and European "multipolarity" – if it foolishly makes a play for Eurasia. And since it can't dominate Eurasia, it won't really threaten America by controlling the resources of this global heartland. Yet the argument somehow dismisses the whole question of whether multipolarity will, in time, work against China's interests in the Indo-Pacific, where within a few decades the combined economic, population and military weight of India, Japan, Australia and Indonesia could, without America, be larger than China's. Hugh claims that China and India can avoid a clash of interests because China will leave the Indian Ocean as a sphere of interest for India. This requires erasure of the inconvenient fact of Xi's signature external policy, the Belt and Road Initiative, which involves dominance of ports, undersea cables and other economic infrastructure across the two oceans, Eurasia and beyond. None of this means that India will line up militarily against China in a war over Taiwan – one of Hugh's favourite straw men is to claim that some of us imagine India alone will save the day.

But it does mean that China courts a widening horizon of risk and is provoking balancing coalitions across Indo-Pacific and global landscapes it cannot dominate. All this widens the aperture for more creative and expansive Australian policy – including multilateral engagement with Southeast Asia, support for Pacific and Indian Ocean island countries grounded in more than our own security fears, and, yes, judicious dialogue with China based on coexistence, mutual interest and an attempt at mutual respect. On that vision, perhaps Hugh and I can agree – though there's no need to prematurely surrender Taiwan to get there.

Rory Medcalf

SLEEPWALK TO WAR

Correspondence

Emma Shortis

I am far from the first to point out that Hugh White is a critical figure in what is, for the most part, an embarrassingly shallow and unimaginative national "debate" about Australia's relationship with China and Australian foreign policy more broadly. *Sleepwalk to War* builds on White's longstanding efforts to bring rigour and self-reflection to both the discussion and the practical implementation of Australian foreign and security policy. The essay, and the initial responses to it, only further demonstrate that too often White is an almost singular voice of dissent in a stale consensus.

White faces the most pressing questions of Australia's place in the world head-on: questions like the strategic importance of Taiwan to both the United States and to Australia, the reliability of Australia's greatest and most important ally, and how a conflict might go nuclear. Despite a dramatically changed domestic political environment, honest answers to these critical questions – even the act of posing them – are both rare and desperately needed.

Unsurprisingly, it is these vital problems that are the focus of most of the responses to White's timely intervention. Even as White identifies "a serious and systemic failure of our intelligence, defence and foreign policy establishments, and the penumbra of think-tanks and university departments that surround them," the responses (with obvious exceptions) take White's analysis and critique seriously, treating it with the respect it deserves – even as most of them come from the same institutional environments White criticises (just as, it must be said, both White and I do). White has, as usual, prompted a flurry of debate about policy and diplomacy among those same circles – even though one suspects that, in the end, most of his critique will be dismissed.

These immediate policy debates, urgent as they are, also obscure the "serious and systemic" failures White rightly pinpoints. At the same time, they reveal just who gets to dissent, and be taken seriously when they do. White argues that there is a pressing need for a "national conversation" about Australia's place in the world – one that is both broader and deeper than the current discourse.

So why aren't we having one? And why have we failed so badly?

The answers to those questions, I think, lie at least partly in the pronouns. Who, exactly, is the "we" that those of us in these institutional settings refer to when discussing Australian foreign policy and its history? Who is the "we" that White argues "failed" collectively to anticipate British abandonment in the mid-twentieth century, and how did it come to be "*our* fault that we did not take more responsibility for our own security as a result" (emphasis added)?

In fact, those failures are the responsibility of a very specific set of very powerful people making particular choices, as is the collective, self-reinforcing failure to reckon with them. And these failures are foundational.

National "conversations" about Australia's unwillingness to "take responsibility for our own security" rarely interrogate why it is that "we" as a nation have consistently turned to bigger white governments to provide that security. They do not generally acknowledge that at least some of Australia and the United States' "shared values" stem from our shared histories as nations founded on dispossession and attempted genocide, or that successive governments of both nations have, so far at least, refused to really confront that history. That history and those "shared values" must be taken into consideration in any analysis of the "threat" posed by a rising China. When "we" express concern about living under the shadow of China, what exactly are "we" worried about? White's radical assertion that there is a "clear possibility that China will turn out to be a regional hegemon we can learn to live with" deserves much more attention than it will get in mainstream discussions, precisely because it would require profoundly complex interrogations of racism, machismo and history that do not preclude similarly complex debates about the way "we," as a nation, are committed to upholding and supporting democracy and human rights. As White implicitly suggests, an Australian foreign policy based on such a deep commitment would look very different to what we have now, and it would involve a dramatic re-evaluation of Australia's alliance with the United States.

That relationship – one that White has critiqued for a long time – sits at an inflection point. White is right when he argues that "our ally will probably fail us," but I don't think he goes far enough. The collapse of American democracy is a real possibility. What would *that* failure look like? How could, and should, "we" as a nation respond?

These potential and foundational failures also point to the discipline of International Relations' troubled relationship with History. History, while lauded (is it even an essay on international relations if it doesn't mention Thucydides?), becomes not a source of imagination but a constraint on the possible. Security alliances and strategic, rational thought become the expected norm, as does the rise and fall of hegemons and changing balances of power. The fine-grained historical analysis that we need, and which informs much of White's essay, goes missing. It is in that detailed, delicate analysis, in the honest recognition of our shared, messy histories, that we might find the imagination and the ambition required for more than just avoiding war. We might aspire instead to a genuine and inclusive peace in which we all prosper, together, and to a fundamental role for this nation in building it.

Emma Shortis

SLEEPWALK TO WAR

Correspondence

Dennis Altman

Generals, it is said, tend to fight the last war. There are echoes of this in the growing anxieties about Australia's security, with references to the dangers of appeasement and Japanese aggression in World War II. Fear of a potential Chinese base in Solomon Islands draws on memories of the battle for Guadalcanal in 1943, when US forces began driving back the Japanese advance.

The American alliance has been the bedrock of Australian security planning since World War II, leading us into wars in Vietnam, Afghanistan and Iraq, and to ever-deepening integration into US military planning. It is the central and most significant insight in Hugh's essay that this alliance may pose considerable dangers to Australian security, increasing rather than diminishing the possibility of major conflict in what politicians now like to call the Indo-Pacific.

The new federal government is trying to balance commitment to the United States with greater attention to both the Pacific and Southeast Asia, although Albanese's attendance at the recent NATO summit suggests it shares the dominant paradigm of a global contest between democracies and autocracies. There is some truth to this, but it also ignores the realities of strongly held nationalist grievances. There is a parallel to the way in which the United States and Australia misunderstood the importance of nationalism in Vietnam, seeing the North Vietnamese communists as, to quote Robert Menzies, "part of a thrust by Communist China between the Indian and Pacific Oceans."

Anxieties about a new Cold War have been heightened by the Russian invasion of Ukraine, which echoes centuries-old disputes over territory that at various times has been part of Lithuania, Austria-Hungary and Russia. The conflict is more than simply a vanity project of Vladimir Putin: there is a deep connection between Russia and much of what is now Ukraine, symbolised for many Russians by the city of Odessa, essentially founded by Catherine the Great and immortalised in Eisenstein's images of the city steps in his film *Battleship Potemkin*.

To acknowledge history is not to excuse current outrages, but it is necessary to understand why many Russians support the invasion. In the same way, the Chinese claim to Taiwan is based on centuries of Chinese control and bitter memories of the civil wars of last century, when the Nationalist government of Chiang Kai-shek fled to the island. Until 1972 both the United States and Australia recognised his government as that of China, so we can hardly be surprised if the Chinese government believes it has a legitimate claim to the island.

Media commentators in Australia seem surprised that major Third World countries, such as India, Brazil and South Africa, have not joined in condemnation of Russia. The majority of countries in the world – and in our region – have a realistic appraisal of China's rise and are seeking to find ways of balancing one great power against another. They might well provide a better guide for Australian policy-makers than the hawks of Washington.

It is certainly possible that China may try to take back Taiwan by force, but this does not mean that it is likely to attempt military conquests beyond what it regards as its legitimate territory. Rather, it will behave as other great powers have in using a range of military, economic and political pressures to suit its national interests. The complaint that China is breaking the "rules-based international order" would be more persuasive had the United States not so frequently disregarded these rules.

Hugh has long argued that Australia needs to become more self-sufficient in defence planning, which makes his scepticism about the AUKUS agreement all the more telling. I would only add that the images of Scott Morrison flanked by Joe Biden and Boris Johnson reinforced the perception of many in our region that Australia still longs for a world ruled by white imperial powers, a dangerous delusion for a country situated in the Indo-Pacific region. Penny Wong is clearly aware of these perceptions, as she made clear in stressing that Australians are "more than just supporting players in a grand drama of global geopolitics" at a G20 meeting of foreign ministers.

The disquiet within the region about Australia's plans for nuclear submarines, expressed most clearly by Malaysia, suggests that there is a cost beyond the astronomical amount required to build, purchase and operate the ships. Labor's rush to endorse the project was understandable in the lead-up to an election. Now that it holds power, one hopes it will ponder Hugh's warnings about the problems of the arrangement.

Many years ago, then trade minister Neal Blewett remarked that Australia needs to be particularly agile diplomatically as we belong to no obvious bloc. It is difficult to imagine us as a member of ASEAN, and rhetoric about "the Pacific family" disguises that we are essentially a neo-colonial power, albeit largely benevolent. For a small fraction of our military expenditure, Australia could increase its diplomatic presence, which Lowy Institute research has shown lags behind that of most comparable countries.

As Hugh points out, Morrison's claim that our alliance with the United States and the United Kingdom is a "forever partnership" ignores the harsh reality that countries will act according to their perception of national interest at any given moment. With the possibility of a return to power by Trump, or by a Republican in the Trump mould, our reliance on the United States becomes more dangerous. (In my first draft I typed "Untied States," which is increasingly appropriate.) In pointing to the flaws of the AUKUS agreement, Hugh is echoing comments in September 2021 by Paul Keating, who diagnosed "a monster level of incompetence."

Hugh's essay is a powerful antidote to the excessive dependence on the United States, which is increasing even as that country becomes internally more divided and isolationist. While politicians rail against Chinese influence in our universities, the University of Sydney hosts a large US Studies Centre that increasingly positions itself as a booster of the American alliance. Many years ago, when I sat on its advisory committee, I suggested that a key research question was to evaluate the benefits of the alliance; that question went unanswered.

A world dominated by China is not an attractive proposition, one that is worth working to prevent. But to do this requires skilful diplomacy and an acceptance that neither we nor the United States can prevent its rise as the predominant military and economic power in East Asia. As Hugh points out, there are "profound moral imperatives" as we balance values and principles against the imperative to avoid war. "Peace," he reminds us, "is a value too."

It is possible that Russia's slow advance in Ukraine, following the ignominious withdrawal of the United States from Afghanistan, suggests that military interventions of this sort are relics of a dying world. In a recent article in *The New York Review of Books* Sophie Pinkham writes that Russia's attack "begins to look like the convulsion of a dying state," asserting that massive climate change is eroding Russia's internal stability.

Pinkham's essay reminds us that we need a more fundamental re-evaluation of Australia's security interests than Hugh's essay suggests. His argument rests on an assumption that China's rise presents the greatest challenge to Australia's security. Yet over the past few years the realities of climate change and new epidemic diseases have been far greater assaults on national security than Chinese trade embargoes and cyber interference.

If scientific forecasts are correct, the AUKUS submarines will be delivered into a very different world to the current one, a world in which fire, flood, pestilence, food shortages and massive refugee flows will present real and present dangers. It is easier to envision enormous social, economic and political upheavals in our part of the world as consequences of non-military disasters than it is to imagine a Chinese military attack on Australia.

The scale of such upheavals will require us to work with the Chinese government, however repugnant its domestic repressions. Were the Republicans to control US politics after 2024, this would produce the greatest strain on our alliance since the Whitlam government, so well described in James Curran's *Unholy Fury*. If the Albanese government is serious about making climate change a crucial element of its approach to domestic and foreign policy, how would it respond to a United States that refused to accept the Paris Agreement? We already know that climate change is a central concern for Pacific island nations. Faced with a choice between China and Trump's America, should we be surprised were they to favour Beijing?

Dennis Altman

SLEEPWALK TO WAR

Response to Correspondence

Hugh White

The first thing that strikes me about these interesting responses to Quarterly Essay 86 is that, despite wide differences of tone, most share a strong assumption that everything will work out fine. They exude confidence that China's ambitions can be easily contained, that America will remain a major strategic power in Asia, that the risk of war is manageable and acceptable, that Australia's current policy settings are broadly right, and that our future in Asia will therefore not be very different from what we have known.

I'm reminded of something that Keynes once wrote: "The idea of the future being different from the present is so repugnant to our conventional modes of thought and behaviour that we, most of us, offer a great resistance to acting on it in practice." The deepest reason that I take a more pessimistic view of these matters is that I think the future is going to be very different from the present – or rather, that the present is already very different from the past – in one absolutely fundamental way. In the past, America was by far the richest and most powerful country in the world, and China was a lot poorer and weaker. Today, China's economy is already bigger than America's on the most relevant measure. That changes everything. It makes it much harder for America to retain a strategic position in East Asia, and much easier for China to push it out. It makes it much harder to deter China from confronting America militarily. It makes it much less likely that we can depend on America as the foundation of our security the way we have done for so long.

It is significant that so many of these commentaries – five of them, in fact – argue that one key reason to reject my pessimistic view of our current situation is that China's economy is likely to falter, and that China's ambitions to take America's place as the leading regional power will falter with it. There are three broad reasons to reject this argument. The first is a point about prudently learning from our mistakes, because we have got this wrong before. For thirty years, Western policy-makers and analysts have consistently predicted that China's economic growth is about to stall. Of course, this time they might be right, but we should be careful of presuming that they are. It is tempting to evade hard choices and unwelcome truths by assuming that the Chinese will solve our problems for us by screwing up. But the only prudent basis for policy is to expect them to succeed.

The second, more powerful reason to reject faint hopes of future Chinese failure is that the horse has already bolted. The shift in wealth and power has *already* happened. China is far wealthier and stronger relative to America than the Soviet Union ever was at its peak, and it is already strong enough to raise the costs and risks to America of resisting its ambitions to the point that they exceed America's imperatives to do so. So whether China's economy stagnates in the years ahead doesn't make much difference.

The third reason is that the optimists don't have to take my word for it. The figures I quoted on the first page of the essay are not mine. They are the Australian government's. They say that today China's economy is 19 per cent of global GDP and America's is 16 per cent, and that by 2035 China will be at 24 per cent and America just 14 per cent. These numbers tell us that the future will not be like the past, and the refusal of our government and so many commentators to accept that simple, essential fact explains why we are failing to address the biggest foreign policy challenge we have faced since 1788.

Part of that failure is a refusal to recognise the risks of war and how those risks should shape our policy. None of these commentaries directly engages with what is, I suppose, the starkest judgment in the essay: that Australia should declare that we will not go to war with China to defend Taiwan, and that we should urge America to do the same. This proposition is central to the essay. The question it addresses is not in any way hypothetical, because the risk that China will move against Taiwan militarily is high and fast getting higher. The clear trend of both Australian and US policy has been to affirm that we should and would go to war to defend Taiwan if China attacks. And no one here contests my argument that such a war not only could not be won, but would also probably go nuclear. The challenge for those who believe that we should maintain our current policy is to explain why we should be willing to fight such a war, and what we could hope to gain. The choice we face about this is extraordinarily difficult, of course, but I do not think we can chart our course in Asia over the years to come without confronting it and answering it.

Rory Medcalf sidesteps this challenge by arguing that war will be avoided because confrontations will be limited to the "grey zone" below the level of conventional warfare. His main reason for thinking this is that the contest has remained in the grey zone until now – for example, in the South China Sea. That is true, of course, but is it reassuring? Rory thinks it is, because he assumes that Beijing has been unwilling to escalate to military conflict. On the contrary, it has been Washington's reluctance to risk a war with China that has kept the confrontations in the grey zone. That is why America has been unable to stop China making gains in the South China Sea. If it is to contain China's challenge, Washington will eventually – and sooner rather than later – have to step up and meet Beijing's grey-zone provocations by escalating to a military confrontation, whether over Taiwan or some other issue. War between the US and China is not inevitable, but with the stakes so high it will only be avoided if one side backs off. And when China's stake is so plainly higher than America's – because we are talking about China's backyard – it is pure wishful thinking to assume that it will be China that backs off.

Of course, they might both back off. This is the possibility encompassed by the idea – promoted by several of these commentaries – that the future we need to prepare for is not Chinese regional hegemony but multipolarity. That is half-right. As I argue in the essay, China will not be able to establish a sphere of influence over Asia as a whole because it will not be able to dominate India. Instead, India will assert its own sphere of influence south and west of the Malacca Straits, so we will find ourselves in a bipolar Asia. But it is wishful thinking to assume that China cannot establish primacy in East Asia and the Western Pacific if it can push America out of the region. Its potential rivals in East Asia are too weak to counterbalance it. Japan by 2035, on Canberra's own estimates, will have an economy only one-sixth the size of China's. It will be strong enough to look after itself, but not to look after anyone else. And by 2035, Indonesia's economy will be about the same size.

But will America be pushed out of the region? Sam Roggeveen and Peter Varghese both suggest that America will not be pushed out of Asia, but will remain a key strategic player in East Asia in some kind of multipolar regional order. There is a lot of talk about multipolarity these days, but it is more properly applied to the global, rather than the regional, order. I think a multipolar global order is emerging, in which a handful of major powers will compete and balance one another to prevent any of them dominating the world. But each of those major global powers will tend to dominate in its own region, producing a series of hegemonic orders at the regional level – including China in East Asia and the Western Pacific. There is no doubt that the rest of us would prefer a multipolar East Asian order, but that doesn't mean it will happen, because it depends not just on what we would like but on what China wants, and how badly it wants it. Peter Varghese, in a characteristically subtle and compelling contribution, says that China might accept a continuing US role as long as it achieves what it wants: "China at the top and an expectation that all other states would pre-emptively concede the primacy of China's core interests." But what kind of role does that leave America? I think it is clear that China is very determined to get America out.

Sam Roggeveen has an important point to make in this connection. He has done me a favour by picking me up on my loose use of the word "domination." He is right to argue for more precision there, and I agree that China will only be able to achieve, and will probably only aim for, the weaker "sphere of influence" version in East Asia. But even that weaker version presupposes the exclusion of any rival major powers from its sphere, which leaves no hope that China will tolerate a substantial continuing US role.

But does it matter what China wants, if America is determined not to be pushed out of East Asia? Mike Green thinks it doesn't. He does not doubt that America has the power and resolve to contain China's challenge and preserve US leadership in Asia. He too calls this a multipolar order, but he gives the game away when he describes its purpose as the preservation of the "existing US-led rules-based order." To him, I think, multipolarity is just another name for US unipolarity. And can that be sustained?

I argue that it cannot because, ultimately, the costs to America of resisting China's ambitions in East Asia exceed the imperatives to do so. That's because, in the multipolar global order I've described, China will not be able to dominate Eurasia, and hence will not be able to threaten America directly. Mike simply misunderstands my argument in this point. Like him, I think (as would George Kennan) that Chinese domination of Eurasia as a whole would be unacceptable to Washington. But that does not make Chinese domination of East Asia unacceptable to Washington, especially when the costs of preventing it are so high.

Mike is nonetheless convinced that America is firmly resolved to stay the course in East Asia. He adduces as evidence "the broad consensus of the US policy community and the US Congress." That is the same community that thought invading Iraq was a good idea, that committed America to rebuilding Afghanistan, that tried and failed to prevent North Korea (and, it seems, Iran) getting nuclear weapons, and that was convinced that Russia could be easily deterred from contesting the post–Cold War strategic order in Eastern Europe. In each case, the US policy community proclaimed objectives that America lacked the power and resolve to achieve, without seriously considering the US interests at stake. So we are well advised to judge US strategic policy not on what the folk in DC say, but on what they actually do. And as Mike himself acknowledges, they have not done nearly enough – economically, diplomatically or militarily – to successfully contain the challenge posed by China in East Asia today. Nor is there any sign of that changing. Australians simply cannot afford to take America's commitment and resolve on trust.

The most significant part of Kevin Rudd's wide-ranging commentary on my essay is his defence of the proposal – put forward in his recent book *The Avoidable*

War – for what he calls "managed strategic competition" between America and China. As he makes clear in his comment, this is a series of measures designed to reduce the risk that strategic rivalry will accidently flare into war. That is a laudable goal as far as it goes, but it does not get us very far. As Kevin acknowledges, his proposals do not seek to offer any resolution to the rivalry itself by setting out a viable vision of a future regional order that might reconcile US and Chinese objectives. Nor do they offer any guidance as to how Australia should navigate the decades ahead.

The most significant part of Malcolm Turnbull's equally wide-ranging commentary is his argument that AUKUS has no real strategic significance, because it does not represent any material strengthening of support for America. He is right, of course, that the arrangement embodies no new strategic commitments of the kind embodied in the ANZUS Treaty. But I think he is wrong to think that the arrangement therefore carries no strategic weight. It was clearly seen in both Washington and Canberra as a substantial step towards the closer alignment – indeed, the total convergence – of US and Australian strategic objectives in East Asia. And by surrendering the development and operation of such a vital capability as our submarine force to the United States – which is what AUKUS has done – we have very significantly reduced our room to manoeuvre and our capacity to differ from Washington. Malcolm may smile at the words of the senior US official who reportedly said that AUKUS had locked us into American policy for the next forty years. I think those words were meant quite seriously. How much harder will it be for us now to resist future requests from Washington to deploy nuclear forces on our territory, for example, if we concluded – as we should – that that was not in our interests?

Let me turn finally to three commentaries which differ from the ones I have discussed so far. Kishore Mahbubani, a doyen of Singapore's formidable foreign policy establishment, has been remarkably successful in puncturing Washington's complacency about its position and future in Asia. He certainly understands the scale and significance of the shift in wealth and power towards China and India, and the massive diplomatic and strategic changes which must follow. Nonetheless, he too believes that America will retain a key strategic role in Asia, because Beijing will be willing to allow that, "as long as America doesn't undermine any vital Chinese interest." The problem as I see it is that China will view the exclusion of America from East Asia as a vital interest in itself, just as America views the exclusion of any rival great power from the Western Hemisphere as a vital interest. That is why I cannot share his optimism that we will find a "win-win" outcome in the best ASEAN tradition.

Dennis Altman approaches the questions about Asia's future from a much broader perspective, asking whether armed force and military operations are any longer as central to international power politics as my analysis assumes. He suggests that Russia's disastrous experiences in Ukraine (and for that matter America's in Iraq and Afghanistan) might convince other great powers, such as China, that alternative instruments – economic, diplomatic and so on – offer better and more cost-effective ways to expand their influence and promote their interests than old-fashioned military invasion. I think there is a lot in this idea, even without the lesson of Ukraine. It has long seemed to me that, beyond the special case of Taiwan, the Chinese are unlikely to use overt invasion and occupation to build their sphere of influence in East Asia, if only because it is costly and inefficient. But the special case of Taiwan remains, and so does the broader objective of forcing America out of East Asia. For these tasks, I think, China will continue to see armed force as its primary instrument, and America will likewise see armed force as its primary response. Hence the risk of war is very real.

And finally, Emma Shortis's commentary takes a refreshingly different and distinctly challenging approach to the whole question of Australia's place in the world. I read Emma's recent book, *Our Exceptional Friend*, while writing the essay, and found it a very stimulating test of my assumptions and approaches. Emma's view of America is much darker than mine, but her take on the way questions in our foreign policy interact and resonate with the big questions here at home rang a lot of bells for me. I have long thought that the biggest foreign policy questions are ultimately questions about how we see ourselves. And it has long been clear that we must change as we adapt to changes in our international setting. We have done this before – think of Federation and the abandonment of White Australia – and we will do it again. That is why Emma is so right to say that a lot of the weight in our debate about our place between America and China "lies ... in the pronouns" – in the way we define who "we" are. I see no reason to be frightened of that. And that is why I think Mike Green is so wrong to say, as he does, that learning to live in peace with a powerful China would mean "pre-emptive strategic euthanasia" for Australia. I have more confidence in Australia than that. I think we can create for ourselves a secure and respected place in an Asia which is not dominated by Britain or America. And given the way the world has changed, I see no alternative but for us to try.

Hugh White

Dennis Altman is a vice chancellor's fellow at La Trobe University in Melbourne. His most recent books are *Unrequited Love: Diary of an Accidental Activist* and *God Save the Queen: The Strange Persistence of Monarchies.*

Waleed Aly is a writer, academic, lawyer and broadcaster. He is a lecturer in politics at Monash University and co-host of Network Ten's *The Project*. He is the author of *People Like Us* and Quarterly Essay 37, *What's Right?*.

Michael J. Green is CEO of the US Studies Centre at the University of Sydney and non-resident senior adviser and Kissinger Chair at the Center for Strategic and International Studies in Washington DC. He previously served as the senior Asia policy official on the National Security Council staff in the White House.

Kishore Mahbubani is a distinguished fellow at the Asia Research Institute, National University of Singapore, and is the author of eight books, including *The Asian 21st Century*. He was twice Singapore's ambassador to the UN and served as president of the UN Security Council in January 2001 and May 2002.

Rory Medcalf is the author of *Contest for the Indo-Pacific*. He has been a senior analyst in Australia's peak intelligence agency, a diplomat with experience in India, Japan and Bougainville, a journalist, a defence and arms control adviser to the Australian government, and a foreign policy expert at the Lowy Institute. Professor Medcalf has been head of the National Security College at the Australian National University since 2015.

Sam Roggeveen is director of the International Security Program at the Lowy Institute. His forthcoming book for La Trobe University Press is *The Echidna Strategy: A New Framework for Australian Security.*

Kevin Rudd served as Australia's prime minister (2007–10, 2013) and as foreign minister (2010–12). He is global president and CEO of Asia Society and has led the Asia Society Policy Institute since 2015. Rudd graduated from the Australian National University with honours in Chinese studies and is fluent in Mandarin. He also studied at Taiwan Normal University in Taipei.

Emma Shortis is a historian, writer and commentator focused on the history and politics of the United States. Her first book, *Our Exceptional Friend: Australia's Fatal Alliance with the United States*, was published by Hardie Grant in 2021.

Scott Stephens is the ABC's Religion and Ethics online editor. He is widely published on moral philosophy and has edited volumes of the writings of Slovenian philosopher Slavoj Žižek and Australian philosopher Raimond Gaita. With Waleed Aly, he co-hosts *The Minefield* on ABC Radio National.

Malcolm Turnbull was prime minister of Australia from 2015 to 2018. His memoir, *A Bigger Picture*, was published in 2020.

Peter Varghese is the chancellor of the University of Queensland and chair of Asialink. He is a former secretary of the Department of Foreign Affairs and Trade and director-general of the Office of National Assessments. He has also served as the international adviser to Prime Minister John Howard and as Australia's High Commissioner to India and Malaysia.

Hugh White is the author of *The China Choice*, *How to Defend Australia* and three Quarterly Essays: *Power Shift*, *Without America* and *Sleepwalk to War*. He is emeritus professor of strategic studies at ANU and was principal author of Australia's Defence White Paper 2000.

QUARTERLY ESSAY BACK ISSUES

BACK ISSUES: (Prices include GST, postage and handling within Australia.) *Grey indicates out of stock.*

- ☐ **QE 1** ($17.99) Robert Manne *In Denial*
- ☐ **QE 2** ($17.99) John Birmingham *Appeasing Jakarta*
- ☐ **QE 3** ($17.99) Guy Rundle *The Opportunist*
- ☐ **QE 4** ($17.99) Don Watson *Rabbit Syndrome*
- ☐ **QE 5** ($17.99) Mungo MacCallum *Girt By Sea*
- ☐ **QE 6** ($17.99) John Button *Beyond Belief*
- ☐ **QE 7** ($17.99) John Martinkus *Paradise Betrayed*
- ☐ **QE 8** ($17.99) Amanda Lohrey *Groundswell*
- ☐ **QE 9** ($17.99) Tim Flannery *Beautiful Lies*
- ☐ **QE 10** ($17.99) Gideon Haigh *Bad Company*
- ☐ **QE 11** ($17.99) Germaine Greer *Whitefella Jump Up*
- ☐ **QE 12** ($17.99) David Malouf *Made in England*
- ☐ **QE 13** ($17.99) Robert Manne with David Corlett *Sending Them Home*
- ☐ **QE 14** ($17.99) Paul McGeough *Mission Impossible*
- ☐ **QE 15** ($17.99) Margaret Simons *Latham's World*
- ☐ **QE 16** ($17.99) Raimond Gaita *Breach of Trust*
- ☐ **QE 17** ($17.99) John Hirst *'Kangaroo Court'*
- ☐ **QE 18** ($17.99) Gail Bell *The Worried Well*
- ☐ **QE 19** ($17.99) Judith Brett *Relaxed & Comfortable*
- ☐ **QE 20** ($17.99) John Birmingham *A Time for War*
- ☐ **QE 21** ($17.99) Clive Hamilton *What's Left?*
- ☐ **QE 22** ($17.99) Amanda Lohrey *Voting for Jesus*
- ☐ **QE 23** ($17.99) Inga Clendinnen *The History Question*
- ☐ **QE 24** ($17.99) Robyn Davidson *No Fixed Address*
- ☐ **QE 25** ($17.99) Peter Hartcher *Bipolar Nation*
- ☐ **QE 26** ($17.99) David Marr *His Master's Voice*
- ☐ **QE 27** ($17.99) Ian Lowe *Reaction Time*
- ☐ **QE 28** ($17.99) Judith Brett *Exit Right*
- ☐ **QE 29** ($17.99) Anne Manne *Love & Money*
- ☐ **QE 30** ($17.99) Paul Toohey *Last Drinks*
- ☐ **QE 31** ($17.99) Tim Flannery *Now or Never*
- ☐ **QE 32** ($17.99) Kate Jennings *American Revolution*
- ☐ **QE 33** ($17.99) Guy Pearse *Quarry Vision*
- ☐ **QE 34** ($17.99) Annabel Crabb *Stop at Nothing*
- ☐ **QE 35** ($17.99) Noel Pearson *Radical Hope*
- ☐ **QE 36** ($17.99) Mungo MacCallum *Australian Story*
- ☐ **QE 37** ($17.99) Waleed Aly *What's Right?*
- ☐ **QE 38** ($17.99) David Marr *Power Trip*
- ☐ **QE 39** ($17.99) Hugh White *Power Shift*
- ☐ **QE 40** ($17.99) George Megalogenis *Trivial Pursuit*
- ☐ **QE 41** ($17.99) David Malouf *The Happy Life*
- ☐ **QE 42** ($17.99) Judith Brett *Fair Share*
- ☐ **QE 43** ($17.99) Robert Manne *Bad News*
- ☐ **QE 44** ($17.99) Andrew Charlton *Man-Made World*
- ☐ **QE 45** ($17.99) Anna Krien *Us and Them*
- ☐ **QE 46** ($17.99) Laura Tingle *Great Expectations*
- ☐ **QE 47** ($17.99) David Marr *Political Animal*
- ☐ **QE 48** ($17.99) Tim Flannery *After the Future*
- ☐ **QE 49** ($17.99) Mark Latham *Not Dead Yet*
- ☐ **QE 50** ($17.99) Anna Goldsworthy *Unfinished Business*
- ☐ **QE 51** ($17.99) David Marr *The Prince*
- ☐ **QE 52** ($17.99) Linda Jaivin *Found in Translation*
- ☐ **QE 53** ($17.99) Paul Toohey *That Sinking Feeling*
- ☐ **QE 54** ($17.99) Andrew Charlton *Dragon's Tail*
- ☐ **QE 55** ($17.99) Noel Pearson *A Rightful Place*
- ☐ **QE 56** ($17.99) Guy Rundle *Clivosaurus*
- ☐ **QE 57** ($17.99) Karen Hitchcock *Dear Life*
- ☐ **QE 58** ($17.99) David Kilcullen *Blood Year*
- ☐ **QE 59** ($17.99) David Marr *Faction Man*
- ☐ **QE 60** ($17.99) Laura Tingle *Political Amnesia*
- ☐ **QE 61** ($17.99) George Megalogenis *Balancing Act*
- ☐ **QE 62** ($17.99) James Brown *Firing Line*
- ☐ **QE 63** ($17.99) Don Watson *Enemy Within*
- ☐ **QE 64** ($17.99) Stan Grant *The Australian Dream*
- ☐ **QE 65** ($17.99) David Marr *The White Queen*
- ☐ **QE 66** ($17.99) Anna Krien *The Long Goodbye*
- ☐ **QE 67** ($17.99) Benjamin Law *Moral Panic 101*
- ☐ **QE 68** ($17.99) Hugh White *Without America*
- ☐ **QE 69** ($17.99) Mark McKenna *Moment of Truth*
- ☐ **QE 70** ($17.99) Richard Denniss *Dead Right*
- ☐ **QE 71** ($17.99) Laura Tingle *Follow the Leader*
- ☐ **QE 72** ($17.99) Sebastian Smee *Net Loss*
- ☐ **QE 73** ($17.99) Rebecca Huntley *Australia Fair*
- ☐ **QE 74** ($17.99) Erik Jensen *The Prosperity Gospel*
- ☐ **QE 75** ($17.99) Annabel Crabb *Men at Work*
- ☐ **QE 76** ($17.99) Peter Hartcher *Red Flag*
- ☐ **QE 77** ($17.99) Margaret Simons *Cry Me a River*
- ☐ **QE 78** ($17.99) Judith Brett *The Coal Curse*
- ☐ **QE 79** ($17.99) Katharine Murphy *The End of Certainty*
- ☐ **QE 80** ($17.99) Laura Tingle *The High Road*
- ☐ **QE 81** ($17.99) Alan Finkel *Getting to Zero*
- ☐ **QE 82** ($17.99) George Megalogenis *Exit Strategy*
- ☐ **QE 83** ($17.99) Lech Blaine *Top Blokes*
- ☐ **QE 84** ($24.99) Jess Hill *The Reckoning*
- ☐ **QE 85** ($24.99) Sarah Krasnostein *Not Waving, Drowning*
- ☐ **QE 86** ($24.99) Hugh White *Sleepwalk to War*

Please include this form with delivery and payment details overleaf.
Back issues also available as eBooks at **quarterlyessay.com**

SUBSCRIBE TO RECEIVE 10% OFF THE COVER PRICE

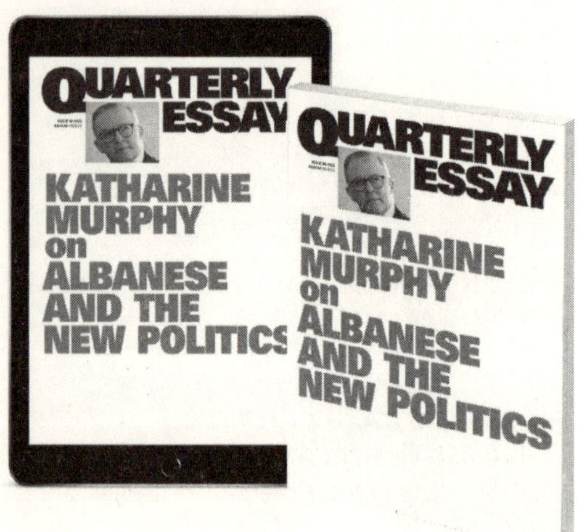

☐ **ONE-YEAR PRINT AND DIGITAL SUBSCRIPTION: $89.99**

- Print edition
- Home delivery
- Automatically renewing
- Full digital access to all past issues
- App for Android and iPhone users
- eBook files

DELIVERY AND PAYMENT DETAILS

DELIVERY DETAILS:

NAME:

ADDRESS:

EMAIL: PHONE:

PAYMENT DETAILS: Enclose a cheque/money order made out to Schwartz Books Pty Ltd.
Or debit my credit card (MasterCard, Visa and Amex accepted).
Freepost: Quarterly Essay, Reply Paid 90094, Collingwood VIC 3066
All prices include GST, postage and handling.

CARD NO. ☐☐☐☐☐☐☐☐☐☐☐☐☐☐☐☐

EXPIRY DATE: / CCV: AMOUNT: $

PURCHASER'S NAME: SIGNATURE:

Subscribe online at **quarterlyessay.com/subscribe** • Freecall: 1800 077 514 • Phone: 03 9486 0288
Email: subscribe@quarterlyessay.com (please do not send electronic scans of this form)